BUILDING FINE FURNITURE

GLEN HUEY

POPULAR WOODWORKING BOOKS
CINCINNATI, OHIO
www.popularwoodworking.com

READ THIS IMPORTANT SAFETY NOTICE

To prevent accidents, keep safety in mind while you work. Use the safety guards installed on power equipment; they are for your protection. When working on power equipment, keep fingers away from saw blades, wear safety goggles to prevent injuries from flying wood chips and sawdust, wear headphones to protect your hearing, and consider installing a dust vacuum to reduce the amount of airborne sawdust in your woodshop. Don't wear loose clothing, such as neckties or shirts with loose sleeves, or jewelry, such as rings, necklaces or bracelets, when working on power equipment. Tie back long hair to prevent it from getting caught in your equipment. People who are sensitive to certain chemicals should check the chemical content of any product before using it. The authors and editors who compiled this book have tried to make the contents as accurate and correct as possible. Plans, illustrations, photographs and text have been carefully checked. All instructions, plans and projects should be carefully read, studied and understood before beginning construction. In some photos, power tool guards have been removed to more clearly show the operation being demonstrated. Always use all safety guards and attachments that come with your power tools. Due to the variability of local conditions, construction materials, skill levels, etc., neither the author nor Popular Woodworking Books assumes any responsibility for any accidents, injuries, damages or other losses incurred resulting from the material presented in this book. Prices listed for supplies and equipment were current at the time of publication and are subject to change. Glass shelving should have all edges polished and must be tempered. Untempered glass shelves may shatter and can cause serious bodily injury. Tempered shelves are very strong and if they break will just crumble, minimizing personal injury.

Visit our Web site at www.popularwoodworking.com for information on more resources for woodworkers.

Other fine Popular Woodworking Books are available from your local bookstore or direct from the publisher.

08   07   06   05   04   5   4   3   2   1

Library of Congress Cataloging-in-Publication Data

Huey, Glen
    Building fine furniture / by Glen Huey.
      p. cm.
    Includes index.
    ISBN 1-55870-645-3 (alk. paper)
    1. Furniture making--Amateurs' manuals. I. Title.

TT195.H8397 2003
684.1'04--dc21

ACQUISITIONS EDITOR: Jim Stack
EDITED BY: Jennifer Ziegler
DESIGNED BY: Brian Roeth
PRODUCTION COORDINATED BY: Mark Griffin
LAYOUT ARTIST: Christine Long
CHAPTER OPENER PHOTOS BY: Al Parrish

metric conversion chart

TO CONVERT	TO	MULTIPLY BY
Inches	Centimeters	2.54
Centimeters	Inches	0.4
Feet	Centimeters	30.5
Centimeters	Feet	0.03
Yards	Meters	0.9
Meters	Yards	1.1
Sq. Inches	Sq. Centimeters	6.45
Sq. Centimeters	Sq. Inches	0.16
Sq. Feet	Sq. Meters	0.09
Sq. Meters	Sq. Feet	10.8
Sq. Yards	Sq. Meters	0.8
Sq. Meters	Sq. Yards	1.2
Pounds	Kilograms	0.45
Kilograms	Pounds	2.2
Ounces	Grams	28.4
Grams	Ounces	0.035

dedication | To my brothers, who were not included in my last dedication. My younger brother, Steve, who desires to create furniture but has moved to bigger and better things — yet still contributes to my business ideas and thoughts — as well as my older brother Mark.

Also to my Dad, Malcolm. We have worked together forever. He has withstood my tirades, acts as a sounding board for each and every idea and continues to give fatherly advice!

ABOUT THE AUTHOR

Glen was born and raised in Ohio. At the age of fourteen he decided to use his father's tools to help build furniture.

Today he is the author of *Fine Furniture for a Lifetime*, a contributing editor to *Popular Woodworking* magazine, participates at shows around the country and has had pieces featured in national magazines. He owns and operates Malcolm L. Huey & Son in Middletown, Ohio. Visit his Web site at www.hueyfurniture.com.

ACKNOWLEDGEMENTS

My thanks to:

My wife, Laurie, who continues to inspire me.

Holly and Jeff Black for opening their home and enduring the "crew" for photo shoots.

Jim Stack and Jenny Ziegler at Popular Woodworking Books for their guidance.

Al Parrish for the wonderful photography.

And to my customers, thank you for allowing me to continue down this path.

table of contents

made in Feb, March 2010

introduction

When I sat down to select projects for this book, I had two distinct ideas. The first was to select pieces that presented a figurative "walk through the centuries." The next thought was to show how, even though we copy pieces and styles, be it from books, museum collections or other cabinetmakers, we all add our own signature to our work.

The collection of pieces shown in this book begin in the 18th century, with the Hanging Cupboard, and progress into today with a few pieces that I have designed, such as the Barber's-Pole Bed. Passing through the 19th century, there is a fine example of Shaker design and craftsmanship, and in the next 100 years we explore the designs of Donald Deskey and James Krenov — shining examples from the past few centuries of cabinetmaking.

The second thought in this book can be discovered in building or studying the pieces included. In the field there is an ongoing discussion on whether a piece is a reproduction or an adaptation. I feel that most pieces of furniture are adaptations primarily because of the tools we use. We build pieces that have our signature: that certain moulding we feel comfortable using, the way we attach a top to a case or the method of building drawers. We put our stamp on our work. If we did not create in this manner, how would the future know this was our work as we today know the work of the Goddards, Townsends, Seymours and Frothinghams?

You will see that I add my "signature" to these pieces, as should you. I had a customer tell me that we should use the term re-creations. I agree.

18TH-CENTURY HANGING CUPBOARD

This piece first caught my eye many years ago. I was particularly captivated by the tombstone style, or arched glass panels in the doors drawing your vision to the display area behind — perfect for showing off your collection of prized antiques.

Believed to be from the first half of the 18th century, circa 1730, and with an association to the Wallace Nutting Collection, this cupboard has a revered history. Although this is a standout selection, it appears to be a stand-alone piece. It is not of a general design.

The ample size and storage, along with a simplistic design, yet challenging construction details, make this a piece that you will want to create.

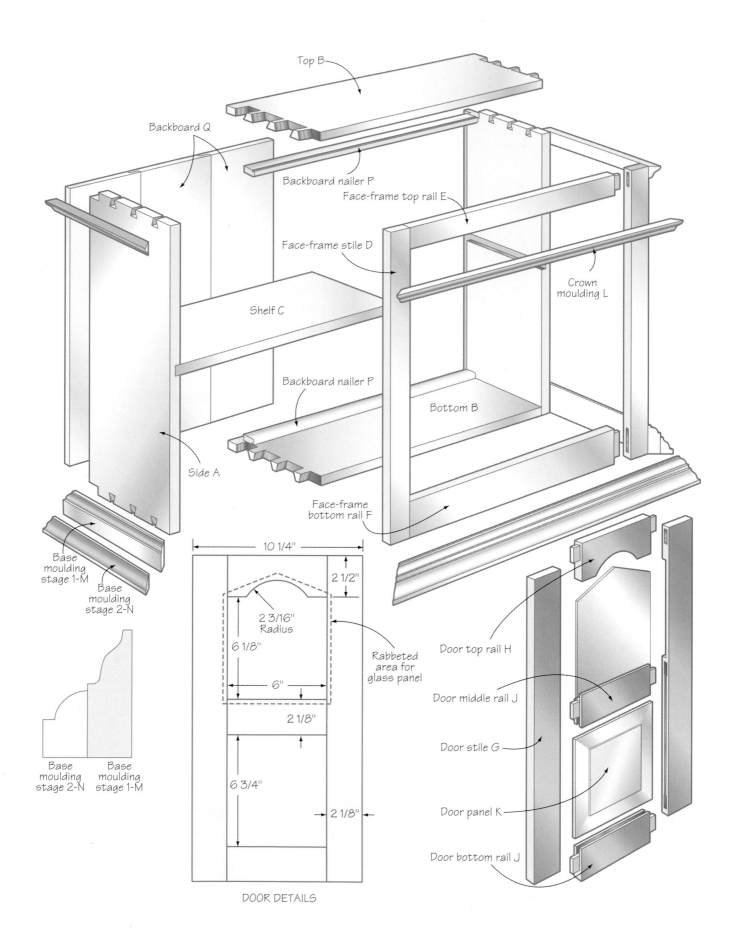

Top B

Backboard Q

Backboard nailer P

Face-frame top rail E

Face-frame stile D

Crown moulding L

Shelf C

Backboard nailer P

Bottom B

Side A

Face-frame bottom rail F

Base moulding stage 1-M

Base moulding stage 2-N

10 1/4"

2 1/2"

2 3/16" Radius

6 1/8"

6"

Rabbeted area for glass panel

2 1/8"

6 3/4"

2 1/8"

Base moulding stage 2-N

Base moulding stage 1-M

DOOR DETAILS

Door top rail H

Door middle rail J

Door stile G

Door panel K

Door bottom rail J

inches (millimeters)

REFERENCE	QUANTITY	PART	STOCK	THICKNESS	(mm)	WIDTH	(mm)	LENGTH	(mm)	COMMENTS
A	2	sides	walnut	3/4	(19)	9 1/4	(235)	24	(610)	
B	2	top and bottom	walnut	3/4	(19)	9 1/4	(235)	24 1/2	(623)	
C	1	shelf	walnut	3/4	(19)	8 1/2	(216)	23 1/2	(597)	
D	2	face-frame stiles	walnut	3/4	(19)	2	(51)	24	(610)	
E	1	face-frame top rail	walnut	3/4	(19)	1 5/8	(41)	22 1/2	(572)	1" (25) TBE
F	1	face-frame bottom rail	walnut	3/4	(19)	2 3/4	(70)	22 1/2	(572)	1" (25) TBE
doors										
G	4	stiles	walnut	3/4	(19)	2 1/8	(54)	19 5/8	(499)	
H	2	top rails	walnut	3/4	(19)	2 1/2	(64)	8 1/2	(216)	1 1/4" (32) TBE
J	4	middle and bottom rails	walnut	3/4	(19)	2 1/8	(54)	8 1/2	(216)	1 1/4" (32) TBE
K	2	panels	walnut	5/8	(16)	5 5/8	(143)	7 3/8	(188)	5/16" (8) TAS
mouldings										
L		crown moulding	walnut	3/4	(19)	3/4	(19)	5 lf	(1524)	
M		base moulding, stage 1	walnut	5/8	(16)	1 3/4	(45)	5 lf	(1524)	
N		base moulding, stage 2	walnut	5/8	(16)	1	(25)	5 lf	(1524)	
P	2	backboard nailers	poplar	5/8	(16)	1 3/4	(45)	22 7/8	(581)	
Q	1	backboard	walnut	7/16	(11)	22 1/2	(572)	23 7/8	(606)	made from various pieces
R	1	door catch	walnut	1/2	(13)	3/4	(19)	3	(76)	
S	1	lock catch	walnut	1/4	(6)	3/4	(19)	2	(51)	

Note: TBE = tenon both ends; TAS = tenon all sides.

hardware

2 pairs	2" × 2" (51mm × 51mm) Wrought-iron butterfly hinges	item #HF-12	Horton Brasses
1	Brass half-mortise cabinet lock	item #LK-9	Horton Brasses
	1 1/2" (38mm) Clout or shingle nails	item #N-7	Horton Brasses
2 pieces	Full-restoration glass, cut to fit		Bendheim
	1/4" (6mm) Square pegs, red oak		
	Button lac shellac		
	Behlen Wool-Lube		
	Olde Century Colors acrylic latex in Brierwood Green		
	Paste wax		
	Glue		
	#0000 Steel wool		

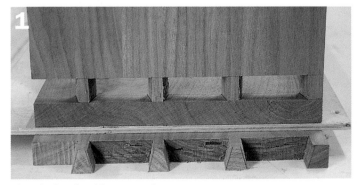

step 1 Cut the sides, top and bottom to size according to the materials list. Then create the pins of the dovetail joint on the top and bottom pieces.

step 2 Cut the corresponding tails into the side pieces.

step 3 With the dovetails complete, cut the $\frac{1}{2}" \times \frac{1}{2}"$ rabbet for the backboards, then locate and create the $\frac{3}{4}"$ dado for the shelf. Assemble the dovetailed box.

step 4 Mill the parts for the face frame and create the mortise-and-tenon joinery to assemble the frame.

step 5 Assemble the face frame, checking to assure that it is square.

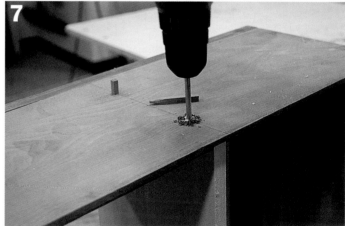

step 6 Using glue and plenty of clamps, attach the face-frame assembly to the dovetailed box.

step 7 Slide the shelf into place and use $\frac{1}{4}"$ square pegs to affix the shelf. I use red oak for the pegs.

step 8 Next, cut the door pieces according to the materials list, lay out the radius on the top rail and create the tombstone effect. Use a $\frac{3}{16}"$ roundover bit on the inside edge of all pieces, making sure to run both edges on the middle rail of each door.

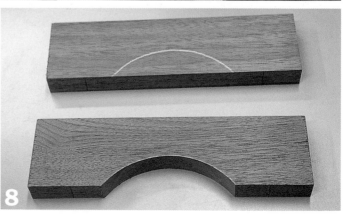

step 9 Lay out the location of the rails on all the door stiles, then cut the mortises as seen on the pieces. Set the saw blade to 45° and cut just to the shoulder of the roundover. There is one cut for each top and bottom rail, and two cuts for the middle rail. The area for the middle rail must be nibbled away and cleaned up with a chisel.

step 10 Use a tenoning jig to remove the waste material where the top and bottom rails meet the stiles.

step 11 Create the same 45° cut in each rail at the required location, then reset the blade to 90° and complete the cut that defines the cheeks.

step 12 Next, adjust the blade height to $^3/_8$" and make the cut that defines the shoulders, remembering that this is a haunched tenon (offset the tenon by $^3/_8$").

step 13 Return to the tenoning jig to complete the cuts for the tenon.

step 14 With all the mortises and tenons finished, set the blade to cut a $^1/_4$"-wide by $^3/_8$"-deep groove on the inside of all pieces and both sides of the middle rail.

step 15 Dry fit the door pieces and make any adjustments necessary. Take the measurement for the panels and cut to size, adding the $\frac{5}{16}$" on all sides. Moving the fence to the left side of the blade, set the blade angle to 12° and make the cut that creates the raised-panel effect. Here you can see that I have raised the blade through a scrap of plywood for safety. The lower edge has to be able to fit into the $\frac{1}{4}$" groove created in the stiles and rails, and not fall into the saw insert throat.

step 16 Glue the door parts and allow to dry. When dry, mark a $\frac{3}{8}$" line (shown here in white) to denote the area for the glass. With a straightedge and $\frac{1}{2}$" pattern bit in the router, remove the waste material.

step 17 This is how the glass area should look when complete.

step 18 Mill the pieces that are to become the case mouldings. The stage 1 moulding for the base is routed with a Roman ogee bit. Cut the miters and nail the pieces to the case.

step 19 Using a $\frac{1}{2}$" roundover bit to form the edge of the stage 2 base moulding, create the piece and nail it to the stage 1 moulding to complete the base moulding.

step 20 The crown is made with a classical ogee bit and simply nailed to the top edge of the case. It's easier to attach the crown when the case is turned upside down on your work surface.

step 21 The backboard nailers are glued and nailed to the top and bottom of the case. Here you can see a groove cut into the bottom of the nailers to eliminate any glue squeeze-out.

step 22 Install the lock into your operable door, then fit the doors into place and install the hinges, making sure to allow equal spacing around the doors.

step 23 Using the biscuit joiner, make a groove in the bottom edge of the shelf, just behind the stile and $\frac{1}{4}$" from the shelf front, to accept the door catch. Next, mark the location of the lock strike and create that catch. It is also possible to purchase an angled strike plate from the lock supplier to eliminate this procedure.

step 24 Cut the stock for the backboards and mill the half-lap joinery for the pieces.

step 25 Remove all hardware and mark each hinge location. The piece is ready to finish. This cupboard is finished with five coats of button lac shellac that is sanded after three coats. After the two additional coats are applied and dry, it is hand rubbed with #0000 steel wool and Behlen Wool-Lube, which aids in smoothing the surface. The interior is painted with two coats of Olde Century Colors acrylic latex in Brierwood Green. Next, nail the backboards into place.

step 26 Install the glass into the doors. Reinstall the hinges into the exact same locations, reinstall the lock and apply a coat of paste wax. Your hanging cupboard is now complete.

SHAKER SMALL CHEST OF DRAWERS

This little Shaker cutie was thought to have originally been built in the Canterbury, New Hampshire, community, although it was found in the Alfred, Maine, Shaker village. The original is from the 1830s and is in a private collection at this time. The antique piece has a painted finish.

This piece was brought to my attention while at a "side-by-side" exhibition where each cabinetmaker created his own version to display alongside the original. Trying to determine which was the original was fun for everyone.

To this day I use my first attempt at this piece as a bedside stand, much as it is shown here.

made it in Feb & march 2010

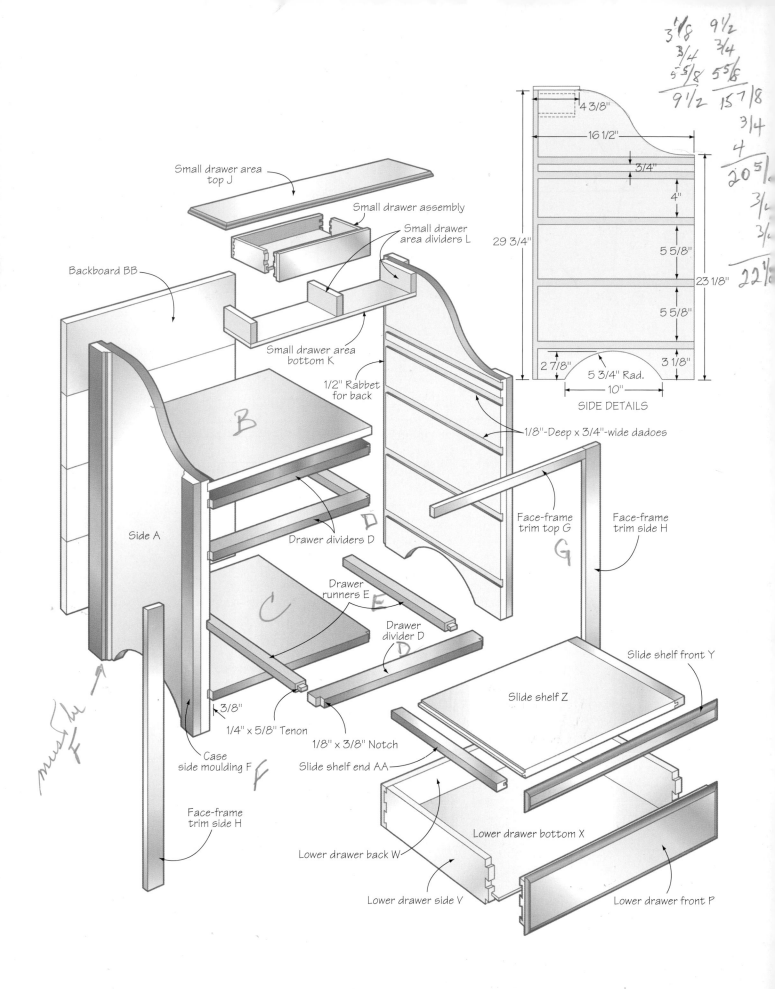

Small drawer area top J

Small drawer assembly

Small drawer area dividers L

Backboard BB

Small drawer area bottom K

1/2" Rabbet for back

Side A

B

D

Drawer dividers D

Drawer runners E

E

C

Drawer divider D

D

3/8"

1/4" x 5/8" Tenon

1/8" x 3/8" Notch

Case side moulding F

F

Face-frame trim side H

Face-frame trim top G

Face-frame trim side H

G

1/8"-Deep x 3/4"-wide dadoes

Slide shelf front Y

Slide shelf Z

Slide shelf end AA

Lower drawer bottom X

Lower drawer back W

Lower drawer side V

Lower drawer front P

SIDE DETAILS

16 1/2"

4 3/8"

3/4"

4"

29 3/4"

5 5/8"

23 1/8"

5 5/8"

2 7/8"

3 1/8"

5 3/4" Rad.

10"

3 1/8 9 1/2
3/4   3/4
5 5/8 5 5/8
9 1/2   15 7/8
       3/4
        4
      20 5/8
       3/4
       3/4
      22 1/8

SHAKER SMALL CHEST OF DRAWERS

inches (millimeters)

REFERENCE	QUANTITY	PART	STOCK	THICKNESS	(mm)	WIDTH	(mm)	LENGTH	(mm)	COMMENTS
A	2	side panels	cherry	$9/16$	(14)	$16^1/8$	(409)	$29^3/4$	(756)	
B	1	top panel	cherry	$3/4$	(19)	$15^1/2$	(394)	$20^7/8$	(530)	
C	1	bottom panel	pine	$3/4$	(19)	$15^7/8$	(403)	$20^7/8$	(530)	strip of cherry at front edge
D	3	drawer dividers	cherry	$3/4$	(19)	$1^3/4$	(45)	$20^7/8$	(530)	
E	6	drawer runners	pine	$3/4$	(19)	1	(25)	$14^1/2$	(369)	$1/2$" (13) TOE
F	4	case side mouldings	cherry	$3/8$	(10)	2	(51)	30	(762)	
G	1	face-frame trim top	cherry	$3/8$	(10)	1	(25)	$20^9/16$	(522)	
H	2	face-frame trim sides	cherry	$3/8$	(10)	1	(25)	$23^1/8$	(587)	
J	1	small drawer area top	cherry	$9/16$	(14)	$4^3/8$	(112)	$22^3/4$	(578)	moulded three sides
K	1	small drawer area bottom	cherry	$9/16$	(14)	$3^3/4$	(95)	$20^9/16$	(522)	
L	3	small drawer area dividers	cherry	$3/4$	(19)	$3^3/4$	(95)	2	(51)	
M	2	top drawer fronts	cherry	$13/16$	(21)	$2^3/16$	(56)	$9^1/2$	(242)	$5/16$" (8) rabbet three sides
N	1	upper drawer front	cherry	$13/16$	(21)	$4^3/16$	(107)	21	(533)	$5/16$" (8) rabbet three sides
P	2	lower drawer fronts	cherry	$13/16$	(21)	$5^7/8$	(149)	21	(533)	$5/16$" (8) rabbet three sides
Q	4	top drawer sides	pine	$3/8$	(10)	$1^{15}/16$	(49)	3	(76)	
R	2	top drawer backs	pine	$3/8$	(10)	$1^7/16$	(36)	$8^{15}/16$	(227)	
S	2	top drawer bottoms	pine	$1/4$	(6)	$2^3/4$	(70)	$8^9/16$	(217)	
T	2	upper drawer sides	pine	$1/2$	(13)	$3^7/8$	(98)	$14^1/2$	(369)	
U	1	upper drawer back	pine	$1/2$	(13)	$3^1/8$	(79)	$20^1/2$	(521)	
V	4	lower drawer sides	pine	$1/2$	(13)	$5^1/2$	(140)	$14^1/2$	(369)	
W	2	lower drawer backs	pine	$1/2$	(13)	$4^3/4$	(121)	$14^1/2$	(369)	
X	3	drawer bottoms	pine	$5/8$	(16)	15	(381)	20	(508)	
Y	1	slide shelf front	cherry	$5/16$	(8)	1	(25)	21	(533)	
Z	1	slide shelf	pine	$3/4$	(19)	$15^1/2$	(394)	$19^1/2$	(496)	$1/4$" (6) TBE
AA	2	slide shelf ends	cherry	$3/4$	(19)	1	(25)	$15^1/2$	(394)	
BB	1	backboard		$1/2$	(13)	$21^3/16$	(538)	29	(737)	made from various pieces

Note: TOE = tenon one end; TBE = tenon both ends.

hardware

3	$1^1/2$" (38mm) Cherry wooden knobs for lower drawers	item #61692	Rockler
2	1" (25mm) Cherry wooden knobs for upper drawers	item #61665	Rockler
2	$1/2$"-dia. (13mm-dia.) Brass knobs with antique finish	item #H-42	Horton Brasses
	$1^1/2$" (38mm) Fine finish nails	item #N-5	Horton Brasses
	J.E. Moser's Dark Antique Sheraton aniline dye stain		Woodworker's Supply
	Reproduction squarehead nails		
	Finish nails		
	No. 8 × $1^1/2$ (38mm) Slotted-head wood screws		
	Screw-hole plugs		
	Lacquer sanding sealer		
	Lacquer		
	Glue		

(handwritten annotations throughout:)
- only 3 cherry drawer dividers
- 2C + 2C ?
- I made it 23"
- 3 3/8
- I used 15" × s/b 20 5/8
- use some plywood
- s/b 1/2" because 19 1/2 + 1/2 + 1/2 = 20 1/2 for slide shelf
- Slide shelf width (depth): Top panel width or depth of unit 15 1/2 / slide shelf front 5/16 ∴ pine slideshelf
- note

step 1 Begin the piece by gluing the side panels. Mark the location for and cut the ⅛"-deep by ¾"-wide dadoes for the top panel, drawer dividers and bottom panel. I use a straightedge with a ¾" pattern bit for this procedure. Make sure you have mirror-image sides.

step 2 Cut the top design, as well as the arched cutouts at the bottom of each side.

step 3 With the drawer dividers milled, set the saw blade to create a ⅛"-wide by ⅜"-deep notch on the front edges of each divider and the bottom panel.

step 4 Next, fit the bottom panel with the front edge, extending the bottom panel ⅜" in front of the side panels. Nail the joint. *glued*

step 5 Fit the top panel into the groove while holding the edge of the panel flush with the sides. Nail the joint with a reproduction squarehead nail. *or glued*

step 6 After cutting the ¼" × ⅝" mortise in the dividers, cut a matching tenon on one end of the drawer runners.

say ½ deep for mortise & ½" long tenon

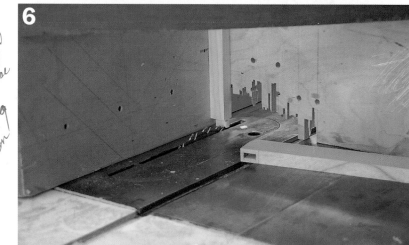

step 7 Install the drawer dividers into the dadoes in the sides and nail, making sure that the nail enters the solid area of the dividers, not the mortised area. *& glued*

step 8 Next, lay the piece on its side and glue the tenon on the runners into the mortise in the dividers. Then place a single nail through the side into the runner, locking it into the dado. *& glued*

step 9 With the dividers and runners in place, set the cabinet upright and cut the case side mouldings to fit. Attach these with glue and a few nails. Here you can see the shallow groove made in the moulding to capture any excess glue, preventing it from spreading onto the sides.

step 10 After attaching the face-frame trim to the top panel with a bit of glue and a few finish nails, measure and repeat the process with both side trim pieces. *glue only*

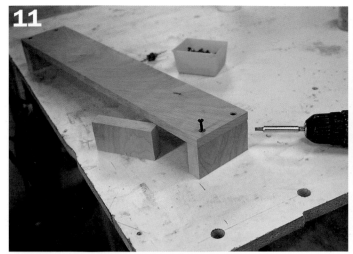

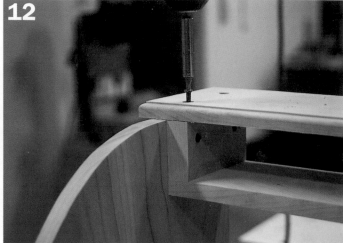

step 11 Take the small drawer area bottom and attach the dividers with screws. One divider at each end and the third at the center equally separate the space.

step 12 Set that assembly in place, bottom down, and using screws, attach it to the sides, making sure that the dividers are flush with the top edge of the sides. With that accomplished, set the top piece in place and attach it, as well. Fill the screw holes with a matching plug.

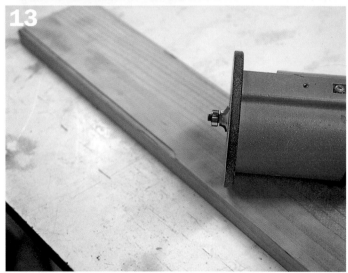

step 13 Mill the drawer front and slide shelf front pieces to size, mould the edges with a $^{3}/_{16}$" roundover bit and create the rabbet detail on the top and sides of the fronts, leaving the bottom edge intact.

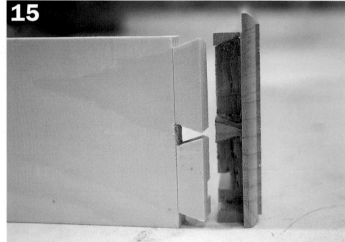

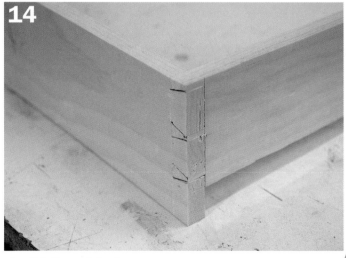

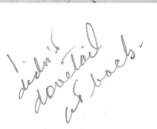

step 14 Dovetail the drawer parts. I start with the back and lay out the pins first. Next, transfer the lines for the matching tails using the pins.

I didn't dovetail at back.

step 15 Repeat the process with the fronts and sides (tails on the sides), then locate the $^{1}/_{4}$" × $^{1}/_{4}$" groove that will accept the drawer bottoms.

step 16 Make the drawer bottoms with the beveled edge to fit into the groove. Cut a blade-wide slot into the bottoms so that it terminates just at the inside edge of the drawer back. Slide the bottoms into place and secure with a nail as shown.

step 17 Mill the slide shelf and create the ¼" × ¼" tenons on the two ends. Create a matching groove on the slide shelf ends, just as breadboards on a table, and attach with nails through the ends. Here you can see that I mill those grooves on a wider piece and then cut to the required width.

used doorskin for bottoms. with a reinforcing strip across the middle, front to back.

— I just glued + nailed sides of cherry on to the pine shelf

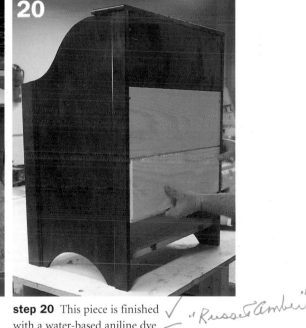

step 18 With glue and finish nails, attach the slide shelf front into place with the bottom edge flush, creating the lip at the top and ends.

did not use router on front. I just rounded it

step 19 Next, make the backboards for the chest, remembering that the top board needs to be made from matching hardwood. It will be seen from the front and should be treated in the finish stages just as the case and drawers are.

cherry boards on top running horizontal. The bottom backboards behind the drawers, were 2 layers of thin cherry plywood

step 20 This piece is finished with a water-based aniline dye stain, J.E. Moser's Dark Antique Sheraton, and when dry, sealed with lacquer sanding sealer, then top-coated with lacquer. The entire piece was sprayed using an HVLP (high-volume, low-pressure) system. With the finish complete, attach the backboards and secure the knobs to the drawer fronts.

"Russet Amber"

was ripped from the 1" cherry lumber to make 3/4" or less parts for the project. These run vertically.

JEWELRY CHEST

In designing this jewelry chest, I particularly enjoyed presenting the contrast. The inverted trapezoid shape is the opposite of what you might expect. It appears as though the piece might tumble if it were not for the gentle curving legs to keep it in balance. The piece is a study of angles, yet there is symmetry in the design, making it soothing to the eye.

I also enjoy the contrast between the hardwoods. The zebrawood with the vertical lines is totally a shock when used as cross-banding on the drawers, but the solidness of the dark wenge calms the overall design.

Have fun with this selection; don't let the contrast get to you!

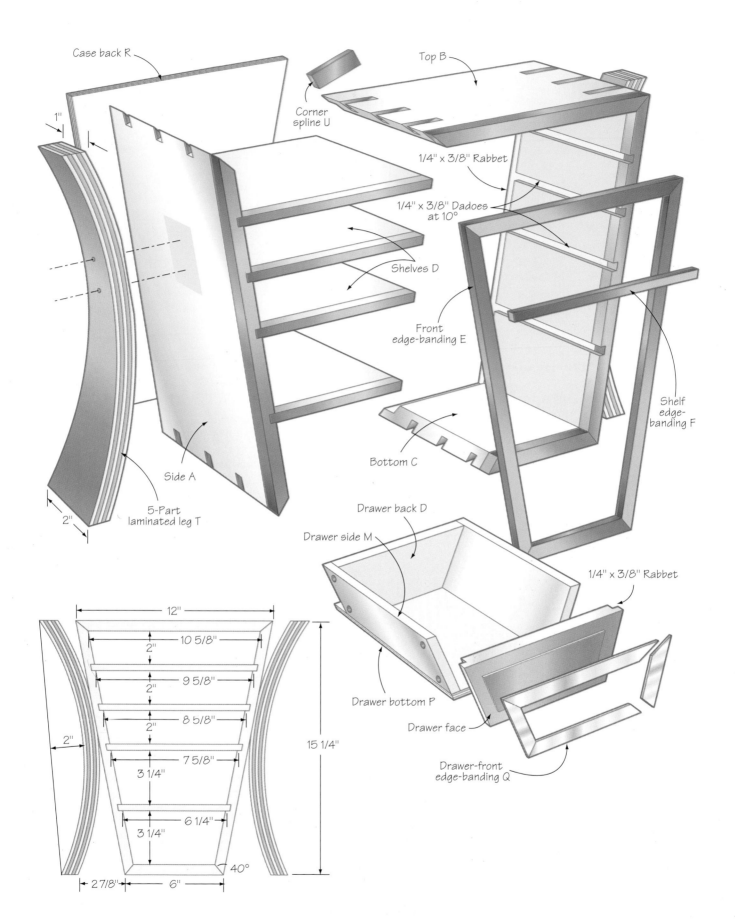

Case back R

1"

Corner spline U

Top B

1/4" x 3/8" Rabbet

1/4" x 3/8" Dadoes at 10°

Shelves D

Front edge-banding E

Shelf edge-banding F

Side A

Bottom C

5-Part laminated leg T

2"

Drawer back D

Drawer side M

1/4" x 3/8" Rabbet

Drawer bottom P

Drawer face

Drawer-front edge-banding Q

12"

10 5/8"

2"

9 5/8"

2"

8 5/8"

2"

7 5/8"

2"

3 1/4"

6 1/4"

3 1/4"

15 1/4"

40°

2 7/8"

6"

inches (millimeters)

REFERENCE	QUANTITY	PART	STOCK	THICKNESS	(mm)	WIDTH	(mm)	LENGTH	(mm)	COMMENTS
A	2	sides	zebrawood	$5/8$	(16)	$5^5/8$	(143)	$15^1/2$	(394)	
B	1	top	zebrawood	$5/8$	(16)	$5^5/8$	(143)	$12^1/8$	(308)	
C	1	bottom	zebrawood	$5/8$	(16)	$5^5/8$	(143)	6	(152)	
D		shelving	zebrawood	$3/8$	(10)	$5^1/4$	(133)	$3^1/2$ lf	(1067)	
E		front edge-banding	wenge	$1/4$	(6)	$5/8$	(16)	4 lf	(1219)	
F		shelf edge-banding	wenge	$1/4$	(6)	$3/8$	(10)	$3^1/2$ lf	(1067)	
G	1	bottom drawer front	wenge	$5/8$	(16)	$3^1/4$	(82)	$6^1/4$	(158)	
H	1	drawer 1 front	wenge	$5/8$	(16)	$3^1/4$	(82)	$7^3/16$	(183)	
J	1	drawer 2 front	wenge	$5/8$	(16)	2	(51)	$8^5/8$	(219)	
K	1	drawer 3 front	wenge	$5/8$	(16)	2	(51)	$9^9/16$	(243)	
L	1	top drawer front	wenge	$5/8$	(16)	2	(51)	$10^9/16$	(268)	
M	6	2" (51) drawer sides	maple	$3/8$	(10)	2	(51)	$5^1/4$	(133)	angle-cut
N	4	$3^1/4$" (82) drawer sides	maple	$3/8$	(10)	$3^1/4$	(82)	$5^1/4$	(133)	angle-cut
P	1	drawer bottom	Baltic birch ply	$1/4$	(6)	12	(305)	30	(762)	
Q		drawer-front edge-banding	zebra	$1/8$	(3)	$1/2$	(13)	as needed		edge all sides of all drawers; use cutoffs from case and shelving
R	1	case back	Baltic birch ply	$1/4$	(6)	12	(305)	30	(762)	
S	2	drawer pins	walnut dowel	$1/4$	(6)			36	(914)	
T	10	laminated legs	wenge	$3/16$	(5)	$2^1/8$	(54)	17	(432)	5 pieces per leg
U	12	corner splines	wenge	$1/4$	(6)	$5/8$	(16)	$1^3/4$	(45)	

hardware

5	Knobs		item #REIB-00	contact Aquabrass.com to find store
	Cyanoacrylate glue with accelerator			
	Felt liner for drawer bottoms			
	$3/4$" (19mm) Brad nails			
	No. 6 x $1^1/4$" (32mm) Square-drive face-frame screws			
	$2^1/2$" (64mm) Drywall screws for making the jig			
	Screw-hole plugs			
	Oil/varnish mixture			
	Wax			

step 1 Glue and cut to size the material for the four pieces of the case.

step 2 Set the saw blade at 40° and make the cuts on the bottom edge of the side pieces, as well as both ends of the bottom piece, while laying the material flat on the surface of the saw.

step 3 Position the fence on the left side of the blade and make the cut for the top edge of the side pieces and both ends of the top piece, creating a chiseled edge on the material. Here you can see that I raised the blade through a scrap piece of plywood in order to better control the work, eliminating any potential problem with the throat clearance.

step 4 Assemble the pieces, check the fit and make any adjustments. Then lay out the shelf locations according to the plan.

step 5 Set the dado blade to a ³⁄₈" cut, tilt the blade to 10° and plow the grooves for the shelves in each side. Set the distance from the fence and cut both sides at the same setting, making sure the sides are mirror images.

step 6 Next, cut the ³⁄₈" × ¹⁄₄" rabbet for the case back.

step 7 Assemble the case with band clamps and glue, and while the glue sets cut the shelves to size, using the case as a guide.

step 8 Make the ¹⁄₄" cuts for the splines to reinforce the angled corner joints (see project nine, step 20 for information and procedure). Glue the splines in place and sand them flush with the case.

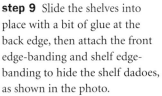

step 9 Slide the shelves into place with a bit of glue at the back edge, then attach the front edge-banding and shelf edge-banding to hide the shelf dadoes, as shown in the photo.

step 10 Next, rip the drawer-front material to size and cut the fronts to fit the case openings. After the fronts are cut, install the plywood case back and nail it into place.

step 11 Mark the fronts and mill the $\frac{3}{8}" \times \frac{1}{4}"$ rabbets for the drawer sides and the $\frac{1}{4}" \times \frac{1}{4}"$ rabbets for the bottoms.

step 12 Raise the blade to $\frac{1}{2}"$ and set the fence $\frac{1}{2}"$ from the blade to create the area for the drawer edge-banding. Cut all four sides of each front.

step 13 Using the cutoffs from the case and shelving, cut $\frac{1}{2}"$-wide strips for the banding. At the band saw, rip those pieces into the $\frac{1}{8}"$-thick banding.

step 14 Fit the banding to each drawer. I used a cyanoacrylate glue with accelerator for instant setting.

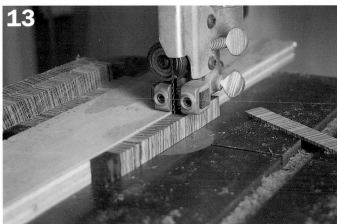

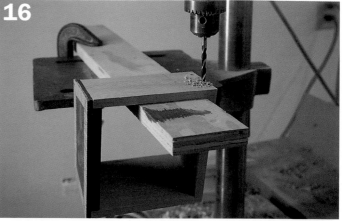

step 15 Mill the remaining drawer material to size by setting the blade angle to 10° and cutting enough stock for both the 2" and 3¼" drawers. Cut the sides and backs. Remember to cut the pieces ¼" less than the drawer fronts to accommodate the drawer bottoms.

step 16 Assemble the drawers. I chose to glue the pieces and then, when dry, drilled a ³⁄₁₆" hole for a walnut dowel for contrast. You may also elect to simply nail the drawers together.

step 17 With the drawers ready, position the bottoms, leaving them a bit long, and nail. Fit the drawers into the case, using the plywood bottoms as stops against the case back.

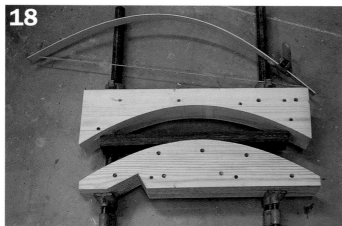

step 18 Using a string and stick jig, set the desired bend for the legs. Make a quick bending jig with two pieces of 2×6 framing lumber and 2½" drywall screws. Create the jig, remembering that the spring back is approximately ½" (overbend the material to allow for the spring back).

step 19 With the leg strips cut to size, apply glue to each matching face and clamp into the jig. Use a piece of wax paper to keep the squeeze-out off the jig. Set this aside until dry and repeat the process for the second leg.

step 20 With both legs laminated and dry, clean the glue from one edge and run each leg over the jointer to make a smooth and true 90° edge to the face. Then set the saw to cut at 2".

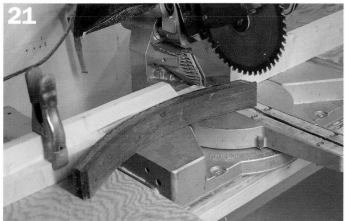

step 21 Set the legs against the case on a level surface, slide a ½"-thick piece of wood up to the leg edge and mark the cut line parallel to the level surface. Set the leg at the miter saw, align the mark with the blade and make the cut while holding the piece in place. Cut both leg bottoms then reset alongside the case and mark the top of each leg equal with the case top. Repeat the cutting steps.

step 22 With the case laid on its back, set the legs against the side and, using a ¼"-thick piece of scrap, mark and cut away an area that will produce a true, flat joint with which to connect the leg to the case.

step 23 With the legs cut to height and fit to the sides, lay out and cut the taper of ½" per side on the band saw, narrowing to the top of the leg. Finish with a light pass over the jointer to clean up the cut.

step 24 Attach the legs to the case with screws and plug the ⅜" holes with appropriate material.

step 25 I finished this piece with three coats of an oil/varnish mixture, allowed it to dry completely, then waxed the entire piece. Finally, add the selected hardware and install felt into the drawers.

t i p | To close up any small gaps between the edge-banding and drawer fronts, apply a small amount of dark wood glue, and sand the surface, allowing the glue and sawdust to mix and fill the spots.

SLANT-LID DESK
ON FRAME

This very early 18th-century desk on frame is an exceptional piece. The original was built in the New England area and is considered by many to be a true masterpiece in design.

With the classic slant-lid desk sitting upon the turned trumpet-style legs as a base, you are naturally attracted to further examine this rarity. As you open the desk, the simple design of the blocked interior catches your attention and you are hooked.

This desk has it all. I was immediately drawn to build this piece. I hope you are, as well.

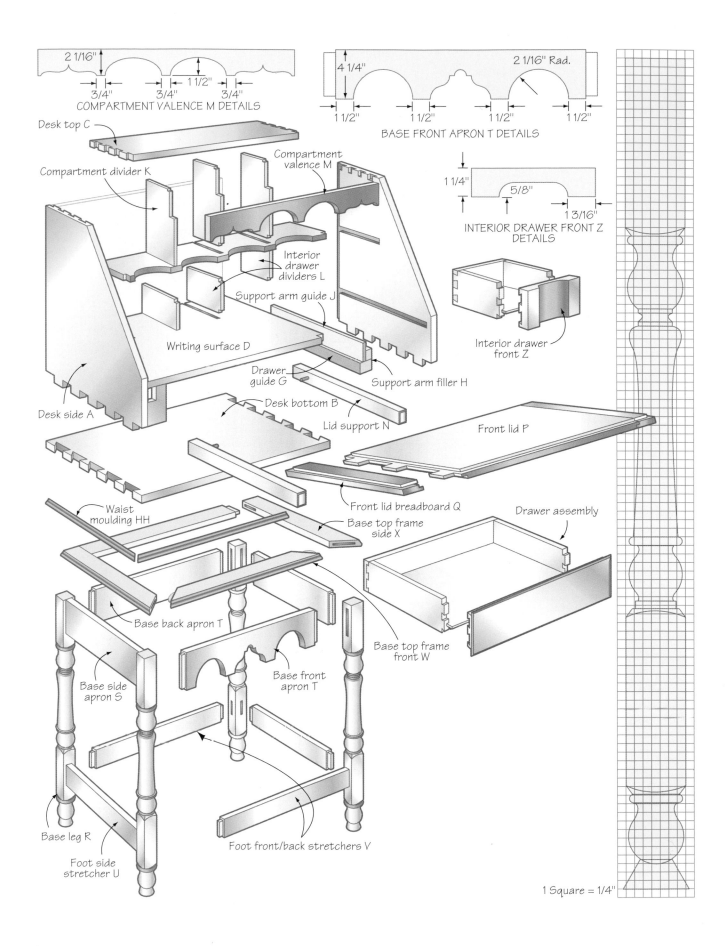

2 1/16"

3/4" 3/4" 1 1/2" 3/4"

COMPARTMENT VALENCE M DETAILS

4 1/4" 2 1/16" Rad.

1 1/2" 1 1/2" 1 1/2" 1 1/2"

BASE FRONT APRON T DETAILS

1 1/4" 5/8" 1 3/16"

INTERIOR DRAWER FRONT Z DETAILS

Desk top C

Compartment divider K

Compartment valence M

Interior drawer dividers L

Writing surface D

Support arm guide J

Drawer guide G

Support arm filler H

Interior drawer front Z

Desk side A

Desk bottom B

Lid support N

Front lid P

Waist moulding HH

Front lid breadboard Q

Drawer assembly

Base top frame side X

Base back apron T

Base top frame front W

Base side apron S

Base front apron T

Base leg R

Foot front/back stretchers V

Foot side stretcher U

1 Square = 1/4"

inches (millimeters)

REFERENCE	QUANTITY	PART	STOCK	THICKNESS	(mm)	WIDTH	(mm)	LENGTH	(mm)	COMMENTS
A	2	desk sides	tiger maple	$3/4$	(19)	$17^3/8$	(442)	18	(457)	
B	1	desk bottom	pine	$3/4$	(19)	$17^3/8$	(442)	$23^3/4$	(603)	tiger maple on front edge
C	1	desk top	tiger maple	$3/4$	(19)	8	(203)	$23^1/4$	(590)	
D	1	writing surface	tiger maple	$3/4$	(19)	$16^3/4$	(425)	$22^5/8$	(575)	
E	1	middle shelf	tiger maple	$1/2$	(13)	$6^3/8$	(162)	$22^5/8$	(575)	
F	2	face-frame dividers	tiger maple	$3/4$	(19)	$1^3/4$	(45)	4	(102)	
G	2	drawer guides	pine	$7/8$	(22)	$1^3/4$	(45)	15	(381)	
H	2	support arm fillers	pine	1	(25)	$1^3/4$	(45)	15	(381)	
J	2	support arm guides	pine	$1/4$	(6)	2	(51)	15	(381)	
K	3	compartment dividers	tiger maple	$1/4$	(6)	$6^3/8$	(162)	8	(203)	
L	3	interior drawer dividers	tiger maple	$1/4$	(6)	$6^3/8$	(162)	$3^7/8$	(98)	
M	1	compartment valance	tiger maple	$3/8$	(10)	$2^1/4$	(57)	$22^3/16$	(564)	
N	2	lid supports	tiger maple	$15/16$	(24)	$1^3/8$	(35)	18*	(457)	size to fit
P	1	front lid	tiger maple	$13/16$	(21)	$15^5/8$	(397)	$21^1/4$	(539)	$1^1/4$" (32) TBE
Q	2	front lid breadboards	tiger maple	$13/16$	(21)	2	(51)	$16^1/2$*	(419)	trim to size
R	4	base legs	tiger maple	$1^3/4$	(45)	$1^3/4$	(45)	$24^1/4$	(616)	
S	2	base side aprons	tiger maple	$3/4$	(19)	$4^1/4$	(108)	$16^1/2$	(419)	1" (25) TBE
T	2	base front and back aprons	tiger maple	$3/4$	(19)	$4^1/4$	(108)	$23^1/2$	(597)	1" (25) TBE
U	2	foot side stretchers	tiger maple	$3/4$	(19)	$1^3/4$	(45)	16	(406)	$3/4$" (19) TBE
V	2	foot front and back stretchers	tiger maple	$3/4$	(19)	$1^3/4$	(45)	23	(584)	$3/4$" (19) TBE
W	1	base top frame front	tiger maple	$3/4$	(19)	$2^3/4$	(70)	26	(660)	45° BE
X	2	base top frame sides	tiger maple	$3/4$	(19)	$2^3/4$	(70)	$18^1/2$	(470)	45° OE
Y	1	base top frame back	pine	$3/4$	(19)	$2^3/4$	(70)	$22^1/2$	(572)	1" (25) TBE
Z	4	interior drawer fronts	tiger maple	$1^1/4$	(32)	$3^1/2$	(89)	$5^5/16$	(135)	
AA	8	interior drawer sides	pine	$3/8$	(10)	$3^1/2$	(89)	$5^1/8$	(130)	
BB	4	interior drawer backs	pine	$3/8$	(10)	3	(76)	$5^5/16$	(135)	
CC	4	interior drawer bottoms	pine	$1/4$	(6)	$4^7/8$	(124)	$4^7/8$	(124)	
DD	1	large drawer front	tiger maple	$7/8$	(22)	4	(102)	$18^5/8$	(473)	
EE	2	large drawer sides	pine	$1/2$	(13)	4	(102)	13	(330)	
FF	1	large drawer back	pine	$1/2$	(13)	$3^1/4$	(82)	$18^5/8$	(473)	
GG	1	large drawer bottom	pine	$9/16$	(14)	13	(330)	$18^3/16$	(462)	
HH		waist moulding	tiger maple	$1/2$	(13)	$3/8$	(10)	6 lf	(1830)	
JJ	1	set of backboards	pine	$1/2$	(13)	$16^3/8$	(416)	$22^3/16$	(564)	trim to size

Note: TBE = tenon both ends; BE = both ends; OE = one end.

hardware

6	$1/2$" (13mm) Brass knobs with antique finish for small drawer and lid support	item #H-42	Horton Brasses	Reproduction nails
1 pair	$1^1/2$" × $2^7/8$" (38mm × 73mm) Antique-finish drop-leaf hinges	item #H-510	Horton Brasses	$1/4$" × $1/4$" (6mm × 6mm) Square pegs
				Drawer stops
2	Antique-finish drawer pulls	item #H-114	Horton Brasses	#20 Biscuits
1	Antique-finish drawer escutcheon	item #H-115E	Horton Brasses	Moser Medium Amber Maple stain
1	Lid lock	item #LK-20	Horton Brasses	400-Grit wet/dry sandpaper
1	Antique-finish lid escutcheon	item #H-114E	Horton Brasses	Boiled linseed oil
	Square $1/4$" (6mm) pins			Blond shellac
	Glue blocks			#0000 Steel wood
	$1^1/4$" (32mm) Slotted-head wood screws			Behlen Wool-Lube
	$3/8$" (10mm) Dowel			Paste wax

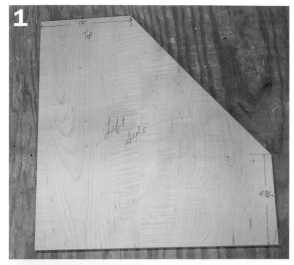

step 1 Begin this project by milling a pair of desk sides for the slant-lid portion of the desk. Identify the sides, making sure they are mirror images.

step 2 Lay out and form the pins on the desk sides, marking the depth to only ³⁄₈". I make sure to end each side with half tails so that I can cut the rabbet for the back without stop-cutting (see step 7).

step 3 Cut the desk bottom to size, shown with the matching hardwood at the front and secondary wood making up the balance, and create a ³⁄₈" × ³⁄₄" rabbet at each end. Place the desk side in position and cut the corresponding tails. This detail allows you cover the dovetails with a small moulding and still keep the strength of the joint.

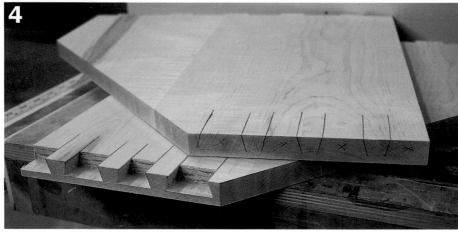

step 4 Lay out and cut the pins on the desk sides for the half-blind dovetails needed for the desk top. Again, leave a half tail at the rear edge.

step 5 Mark the location for the writing surface and create the stop-dado. I like to use a straight-edge and ³⁄₄" pattern-cutting bit.

step 6 Cut the second dado for the middle shelf. Here it is a stop-dado using a ¹⁄₂" pattern bit.

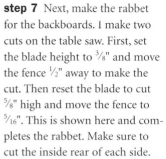

step 7 Next, make the rabbet for the backboards. I make two cuts on the table saw. First, set the blade height to $\frac{3}{8}$" and move the fence $\frac{1}{2}$" away to make the cut. Then reset the blade to cut $\frac{5}{8}$" high and move the fence to $\frac{5}{16}$". This is shown here and completes the rabbet. Make sure to cut the inside rear of each side.

step 8 With your desk top roughed to width and cut to length, invert the sides into place, transfer the layout for the tails and complete the joint.

step 9 Tap the top into place, mark the front edge and cut the piece to its final width.

step 10 Next, back-cut the lower edge of the top with an angle that is 90° to the top front edge, leaving a $\frac{3}{4}$" run at the first cut.

step 11 With the case temporarily together, cut and install the writing surface and middle shelf by notching the front edge to fit the stop-dado cuts made earlier.

step 12 Mark the location of the grooves for the compartment dividers on the writing surface and underside of the desk top. Then use a straightedge to transfer the lines onto the other shelf.

step 13 Dismantle the case and cut the ¼"-wide dadoes for the dividers on the top of the writing surface, both top and bottom of the middle shelf and the underside of the desk top. Remember that all the cuts are stop-dado cuts and the cuts on the middle shelf are stacked over each other so they should be no more than ⅛" deep.

step 14 With the cuts finished, glue the case together.

step 15 While the case is drying, take advantage of the access to install the interior drawer dividers and support arm guides as shown. Attach the drawer guides and the sup- port arm fillers, then glue the front few inches and nail the assemblies into place. Finally add the support arm guides. Do not install the face-frame dividers at this time.

step 16 With the guide assem- blies in place, slide the writing sur- face in and peg the piece through the side with ¼"-square pins.

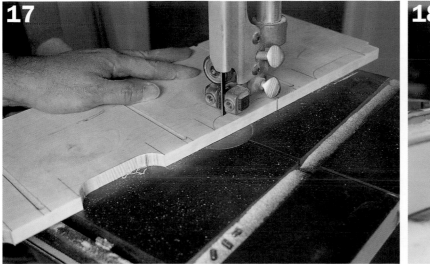

step 17 Next, create the blocked drawer area in the middle shelf. Mark $^3/_4$" from each compartment divider and use a $^5/_8$" radius at each end of the area to be removed. Cut it on the band saw and smooth the surface.

step 18 Slide the completed middle shelf into the case. Measure and cut the interior drawer dividers to fit the stop-dado cuts by notching the front edge at the top and bottom.

step 19 With the drawer dividers fit, cut the compartment dividers the same, remembering to create a second notch at the top to accommodate the compartment valance.

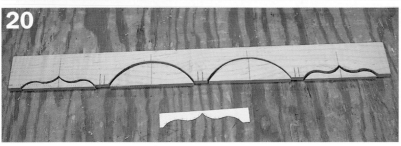

step 20 Fit the compartment valance to the case, then lay out the decorative cuts as shown: Make cyma curves for the outer compartments and radius cuts for the centers, allowing a $^1/_4$" flat on each side of the dividers.

step 21 Install the compartment valance with glue and small blocks.

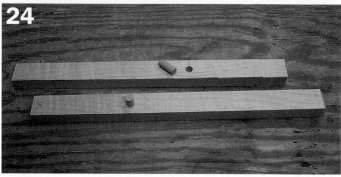

step 22 Next, glue the face-frame dividers into place and complete the installation with a screw through the bottom into the divider.

step 23 Mill the lid supports to fit into their respective areas. Create the beveled end on each support and fine tune the unit.

step 24 Mark the right and left lid supports and then drill for the $\frac{3}{8}$" dowel on the inside face that will act as a stop. Place the hole so that a minimum of 10" extends out from the front.

step 25 Build the drawers. This picture shows the four steps to a finished drawer front. First, mill and fit the fronts in place. Use a small square to align the fronts, and mark the top edge by using the middle shelf profile as a guide. Next, use the table saw to remove as much waste as you can up to the scribe line. Then use the band saw to remove the rounded corners. Finally, sand the area smooth.

step 26 Complete the five drawer boxes. I use hand-cut dovetails and place the bottoms into the grooves set in the drawer sides and front. The bottoms of the interior drawers are attached with brads. In the large drawer, the bottom is nailed through a slot with a reproduction nail.

27

28

31

32

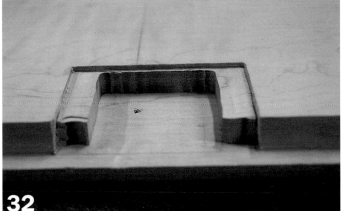

step 27 Mill the parts for the desk lid. Create the breadboard ends by cutting the tongue on the front lid and a $\frac{1}{2}$" groove on the edges of the breadboard ends. (On a piece this size I generally make this cut on the table saw just as you would a tenon.) Then lay out the three extended areas that will accept the square pegs and remove the waste material.

step 28 Transfer the marks onto the breadboards and create the mortises.

step 29 Slide the ends into place, clamp and drill a $\frac{1}{4}$" hole through each tenon. Remove the ends and elongate the outer holes, leaving the center round. Finally, glue the center area and drive square pegs into place, solidly gluing the center and placing glue only at the last $\frac{1}{4}$" of the outer pegs to hold them in place.

step 30 Make the lipped edges on the lid sides. For the top edge, set the blade at the angle matching that of the desk top.

step 31 Mortise the writing surface for the lid hinges. Slide in the support arms, position the lid and transfer the hinge marks onto the lid. Finish installing the lid and hinges.

step 32 With lid installation complete, remove the lid and mortise and fit the lock.

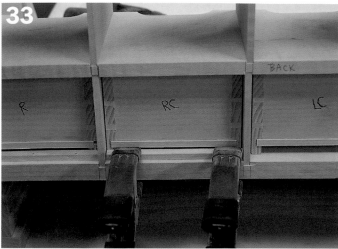

step 33 Glue and tack drawer stops to the back edge of the writing surface to align the drawer fronts with the middle shelf profile.

step 34 Turn the base legs according to the plan and create the mortises for the aprons (leaving a ¼" reveal) and stretcher pieces (in the center of each leg).

step 35 Mill the aprons and stretchers to size, then make the matching tenons and assemble the two sides.

step 36 Lay out the design cuts on the front apron. Make the cuts, sand and finish the assembly of the base section, making sure to square the base.

step 37 Next, mill the pieces for the base top frame. Create the mortise-and-tenon joinery at the rear with 45° angle cuts and biscuits at the front edge. When ready, glue the frame. Once dry, sand the frame and create the moulding profiles.

step 38 Attach the top frame to the base with reproduction nails and glue.

step 39 With the base complete, lay the desk and base on a flat surface and connect the two with 1¼" screws.

step 40 Turn the piece back onto its feet, then make and install the waist moulding. Final sand all parts, and it is off to the finish room.

step 41 I chose to finish this desk with an application of aniline dye (J.E. Moser's Medium Amber Maple). After a light sanding with 400-grit wet/dry paper, I brushed on a coat of boiled linseed oil, which deepens the graining. Next, I sprayed three coats of blond shellac, sanded completely and sprayed an additional two coats. After it sits for a day or two, I rub the finish with #0000 steel wool and Behlen Wool-Lube. Finally, I apply a coat of paste wax.

tip | In making a frame as used in this project, or any frame of this design, it is important to have all pieces sized correctly to ensure that the frame is square. To correctly size the rear piece, cut the front piece to size, then lay out the material needed to create the tenons on the rear piece, as shown. Match the front piece to the rear piece and mark the cut line at the opposite end.

DIMINUTIVE DISH CUPBOARD

If you have been searching for a smaller-size dish cupboard for your home, this is it.

Based on a cupboard believed to have a Canadian attribution from the 1800s, this one-piece cupboard incorporates simple joinery techniques for the case and features a glazed upper door, behind which all your heirloom dishes or collectibles can be displayed for everyone to see. The lower cupboard area has ample storage hidden with two raised-panel doors.

This piece is a keeper whether you finish it naturally or use a painted finish, as I have.

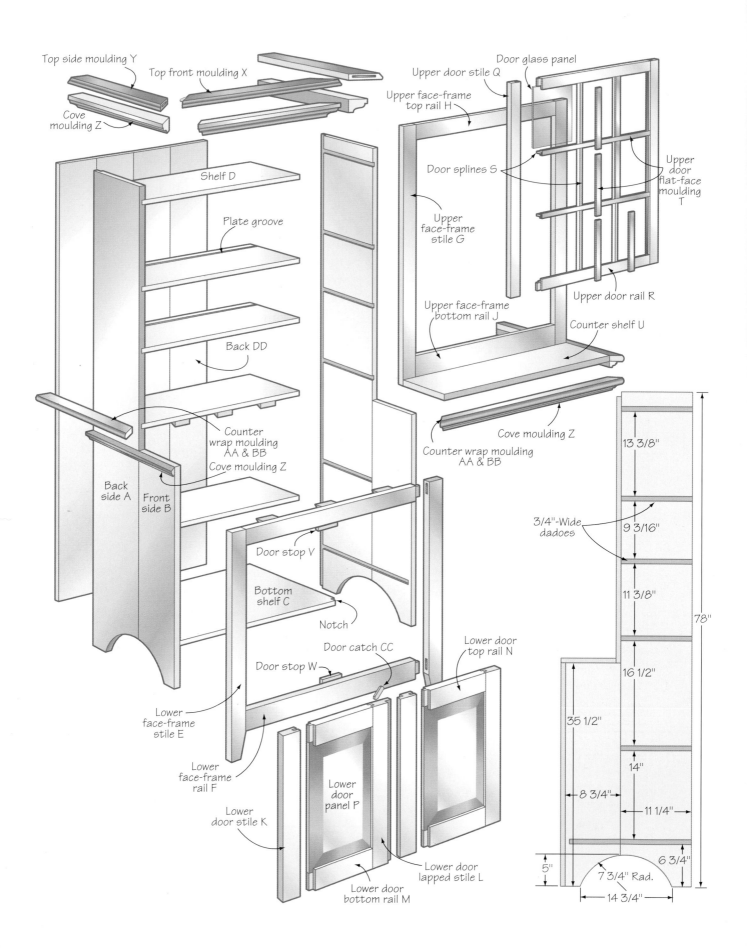

Top side moulding Y

Top front moulding X

Cove moulding Z

Shelf D

Plate groove

Back DD

Counter wrap moulding AA & BB

Cove moulding Z

Back side A

Front side B

Door stop V

Bottom shelf C

Notch

Door catch CC

Door stop W

Lower face-frame stile E

Lower face-frame rail F

Lower door stile K

Lower door panel P

Lower door bottom rail M

Lower door lapped stile L

Door glass panel

Upper door stile Q

Upper face-frame top rail H

Door splines S

Upper face-frame stile G

Upper face-frame bottom rail J

Upper door flat-face moulding T

Upper door rail R

Counter shelf U

Cove moulding Z

Counter wrap moulding AA & BB

Lower door top rail N

13 3/8"

3/4"-Wide dadoes

9 3/16"

11 3/8"

16 1/2"

35 1/2"

14"

8 3/4"

5"

7 3/4" Rad.

14 3/4"

11 1/4"

6 3/4"

78"

inches (millimeters)

REFERENCE	QUANTITY	PART	STOCK	THICKNESS	(mm)	WIDTH	(mm)	LENGTH	(mm)	COMMENTS
A	2	sides (back section)	pine	3/4	(19)	11 1/4	(285)	77 1/4	(1962)	
B	2	sides (front section)	pine	3/4	(19)	8 3/4	(222)	35 1/4	(895)	
C	1	bottom shelf	pine	3/4	(19)	19 1/4	(489)	37 1/4	(946)	
D	5	shelves	pine	3/4	(19)	10 1/2	(267)	37 1/4	(946)	
E	2	lower face-frame stiles	pine	3/4	(19)	4	(102)	25 1/4	(641)	
F	2	lower face-frame rails	pine	3/4	(19)	3	(76)	32 1/4	(819)	1" (25) TBE
G	2	upper face-frame stiles	pine	3/4	(19)	3 1/4	(82)	42	(1067)	
H	1	upper face-frame top rail	pine	3/4	(19)	4 1/4	(108)	33 3/4	(857)	1" (25) TBE
J	1	upper face-frame bottom rail	pine	3/4	(19)	3 3/4	(95)	33 3/4	(857)	
K	3	lower door stiles	pine	3/4	(19)	2 7/8	(73)	24 1/4	(616)	
L	1	lower door lapped stile	pine	3/4	(19)	3 1/4	(82)	24 1/4	(616)	
M	2	lower door bottom rails	pine	3/4	(19)	3 1/4	(82)	12	(305)	1 1/4" (32) TBE
N	2	lower door top rails	pine	3/4	(19)	3	(76)	12	(305)	1 1/4" (32) TBE
P	2	lower door panels	pine	5/8	(16)	10 1/2	(267)	18 5/8	(473)	
Q	2	upper door stiles	pine	3/4	(19)	2	(51)	34	(864)	
R	2	upper door rails	pine	3/4	(19)	2 1/2	(64)	30 1/4	(768)	1 1/4" (32) TBE
S	5	upper door splines	pine	1/4	(6)	1/2	(13)	30	(762)	
T	5	upper door flat-face mouldings	pine	1/4	(6)	3/4	(19)	30	(762)	
U	1	counter shelf	pine	3/4	(19)	8 3/4	(222)	39	(991)	trim to fit
V	1	lower door stop (top)	pine	5/8	(16)	3	(76)	2 3/4	(70)	
W	1	lower door stop (bottom)	pine	5/8	(16)	3	(76)	1 1/4	(32)	
X	1	top moulding (front)	pine	3/4	(19)	3 3/8	(86)	45	(1143)	
Y	1	top moulding (side)	pine	3/4	(19)	3 3/8	(86)	32	(813)	
Z	2	cove mouldings	pine	3/4	(19)	3 1/8	(79)	45	(1143)	
AA	1	counter shelf edge moulding	pine	3/4	(19)	2 1/4	(57)	45	(1143)	
BB	2	counter trim mouldings	pine	5/8	(16)	7/8	(22)	45	(1143)	
CC	1	lower door catch	pine	5/8	(16)	3/4	(19)	5	(127)	
DD	1	backboard	pine	5/8	(16)	37 1/2	(953)	75	(1905)	made up of many boards

Note: TBE = tenon both ends.

hardware

2	1"-dia. (25mm-dia.) Antique-finish cupboard turn knobs		item #H-97	Horton Brasses
1	1"-dia. (25mm-dia.) Antique-finish dummy knob		item #K-12	Horton Brasses
1 pair	2 1/2" (64mm) Blackened upper hinges			local hardware store
2 pairs	2" (51mm) Blackened lower hinges			local hardware store
	1 1/2" (38mm) Case nails		item #N-5	Horton Brasses
	1 1/2" (38mm) Back nails		item #N-7	Horton Brasses
	Full-restoration glass for upper doors			Bendheim
	Glue			
	Glue blocks			
	#20 Biscuits			
	1 1/4" (32mm) Flathead wood screws			
	Cherry aniline dye			
	Shellac			
	Paint			
	Dark wax			
	Durham's Water Putty			

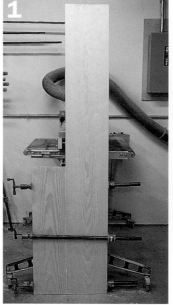

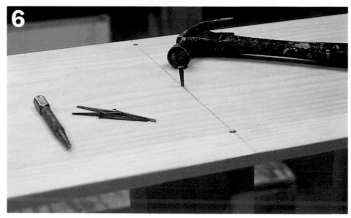

step 1 Begin this cupboard by gluing the pieces for the sides. I used two pieces and cut them so the lower portion was cut straight and located exactly where it is necessary.

step 2 Next, lay out and cut the dadoes according to the plan. Remember that the dado for the shelf in the lower area is a stop-dado.

step 3 After cutting the rabbet for the backboard, mill the shelves to size. For the bottom shelf, notch the front edge to accommodate the stopped cut.

step 4 Apply a small amount of glue in the dadoes and install the shelves.

step 5 Nail through the underside of each shelf, using a square to set the shelf at 90° to the sides.

step 6 Repeat the process on the opposite side and place three nails through the sides at each shelf.

step 7 Mill the pieces for the face frames. Create the mortises in the frame stiles and cut the matching tenons on the rails. Start with the shoulder cuts.

step 8 Finish the tenons by making the cheek and edge cuts.

step 9 With all the joinery cut, glue the face frames and allow them to dry.

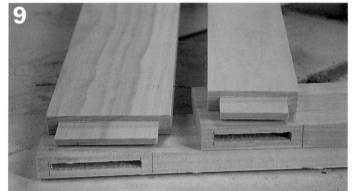

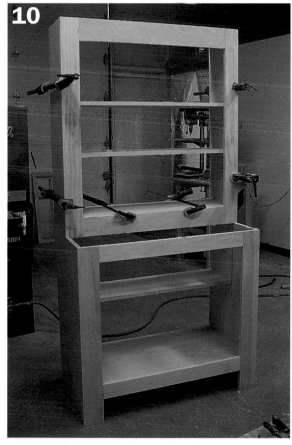

step 11 Mill the counter shelf, fit it to the cupboard and clamp it to hold.

step 10 When they are dry, glue the face-frame assemblies to the cupboard.

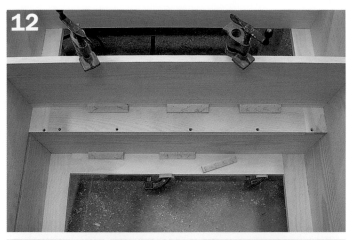

step 12 Place clamps to tighten the upper face-frame rail to the shelf, then turn the cabinet onto the face. Place screws into the back edge of the counter shelf and install glue blocks at the front edges of both shelves.

step 13 Using a ½" core box bit and a straightedge, place plate grooves into the appropriate shelves, 1½" from the back edge to the center of the groove.

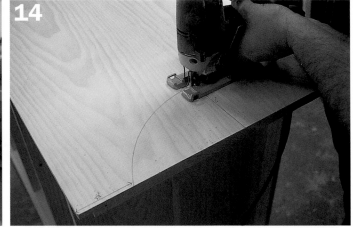

step 14 Next, make the cutout area at the sides and create the angle cuts for the front feet.

step 15 Begin the glass upper door by milling the stock to size, cutting a ⅜" × ½" rabbet on the inner edge of all the pieces. Cut mortises in the door stiles, both top and bottom, and make the face-side shoulder cut on the rails.

step 16 Adjust the fence ⅜" closer to the blade, then make the rear shoulder cut.

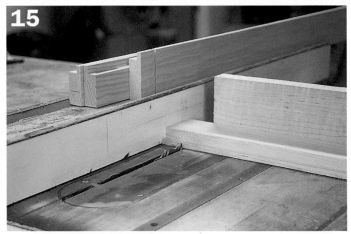

step 17 Raise the blade to ³⁄₈"
and make the outer edge cut.

step 18 Next, make the cheek
cuts, remembering that there are
two different height settings. Remove the haunch area, fine-tune
anything necessary, and the door
frame is ready to assemble. This
method creates the rabbets for the
glass in the joinery. It is also possible to rabbet this area after assembling the door frame with simple
mortise-and-tenon joints.

step 19 This is the front and
back view of the joinery on the
glass door frame.

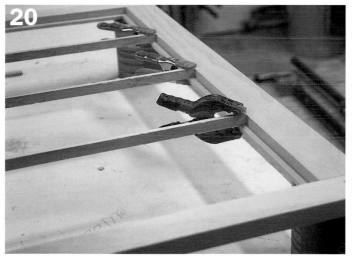

step 20 With the door dry and
pegged, begin the upper door
splines. First, fit the door to the
case and mark the location of
the shelves onto the door frame.
The splines should align with the
shelves. Glue in the splines from
rail to rail, dividing the glass area
into three equal sections.

step 21 Flip the door and install
the flat-face moulding into the
door at each shelf location. Then
simply cut and fill the remaining
pieces to complete the glass door.

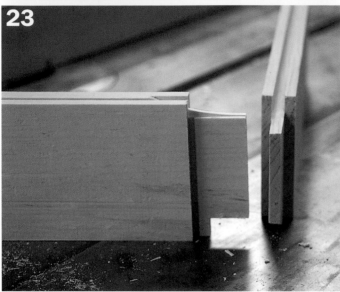

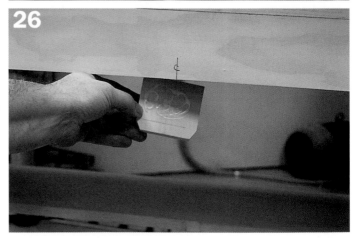

step 22 Next, turn to the lower panel doors. Mill the stock to size and cut the $\frac{1}{4}$" mortises into the stiles, leaving $\frac{3}{8}$" at the top and bottom of each rail width. Begin the tenons by setting the blade height to $\frac{1}{4}$" and cut the shoulder for each rail. Then, raise the blade to $\frac{3}{8}$" and move the fence $\frac{3}{8}$" closer to the blade, just as we did in the glass door.

step 23 Make the cheek and edge cuts, then make a $\frac{1}{4}$" × $\frac{3}{8}$" groove at the center of both the rails and stiles. The end result of the tenons should look like this.

step 24 Mill the panels to size, set the blade at a 12° angle, then, with the fence set to the left of the blade, make the cut to create the raised panel.

step 25 In order to fit the panel to the door groove, you will need to make a $\frac{3}{8}$"-high cut on the inside, or back, of the panel. Test the fit and glue the lower doors when complete.

step 26 Cut the door stops for the lower door, one nailed to the lower shelf and the other as pictured here. Glue them in place and nail from the back to secure.

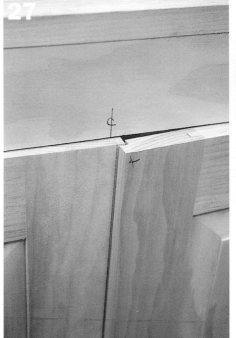

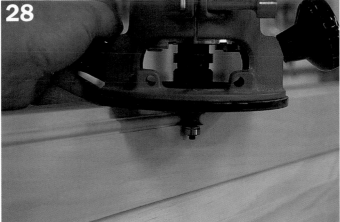

step 27 Hang and fit the lower doors. The operable door (on the right) laps over the other door with a ¼" rabbet. Mark the edge of both doors onto the case to determine the rabbet location.

step 28 Once the doors are complete and fit into the case, remove them and add the bead detail on the outside edge of all stiles. I use a ¼" beading router bit with an auxiliary fence clamped even with the door edge.

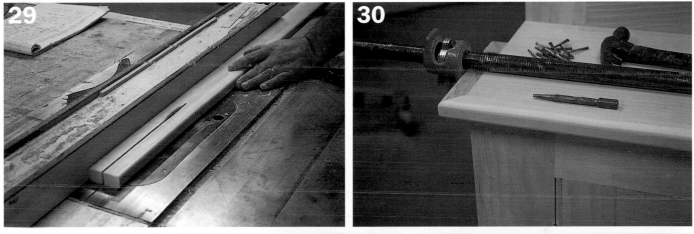

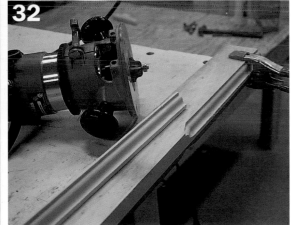

step 29 Make the counter shelf edge moulding by running a ³⁄₁₆" roundover bit on all four edges of the ¾"-thick piece, then rip to the required two pieces that are 1" wide.

step 30 Cut the pieces to size and install the front piece by temporarily clamping a scrap of the moulding at the side.

step 31 With the front piece in place, nail the two sides in the same manner.

step 32 Mill the counter trim moulding as we did the counter shelf edge moulding, using a Roman ogee bit and ripping to size. When you're ready, cut to fit and nail in place.

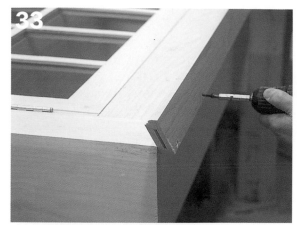

step 33 Next, make the top moulding pieces. These pieces have a moulded edge and are cut to fit with 45° angles that are biscuited at the front corners. They are attached to the case with 1¼" screws.

step 34 Make the cove moulding and fit it to the case.

step 35 Next, mill the backboards and create the ⁵⁄₁₆" × ³⁄₈" rabbet for the shiplap detail. While I sometimes make this with the table saw, here I used the router and a rabbeting bit.

step 36 Sand the piece completely, knock down the edges with coarse-grit sandpaper and send this to the finish room. This is to be a painted piece, but I begin with a cherry aniline dye.

step 37 With the stain dry, apply a couple of coats of shellac. Here I apply a coat of paint that has had fine sawdust mixed into it. Brush it on and as it becomes tacky, remove some paint and most of the sawdust by wiping with a wet rag.

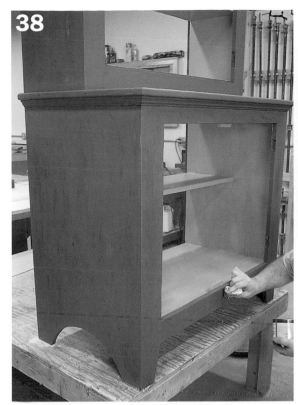

step 38 Paint the interior of the cupboard, and on the exterior add a coat of dark wax to add depth and age to the piece.

step 39 Next, cut the glass and glaze the upper door. I use Durham's Water Putty for the yellowing effect.

step 40 Reinstall the doors. Add the hardware and the door catch in the lower door. Here you see how the catch is attached and works from the inside.

step 41 The backboard is stained on the exterior and painted on the inside. It is nailed using reproduction nails.

t i p | When setting up to cut the glass door grid pieces, I find it helpful to use a new scrap fence with my miter gauge. The piece acts as a backer and the new cut helps to line up your cut.

FEDERAL INLAID TABLE

This highly decorative table will test and improve your inlay skills.
It is based on a Massachusetts piece from 1805 that displays many
of the characteristics of cabinetmakers from that area and period.

The finely turned legs with reeded detail lead up to a scalloped-
edge tray. From there you move up past the exceptional figured panels
toward the drawer front that boasts of mahogany crossbanding and
band inlay that matches the top.

When you finish this table, not only will you have added to your
inlay expertise, you will have created a piece that will be treasured for
many generations to come.

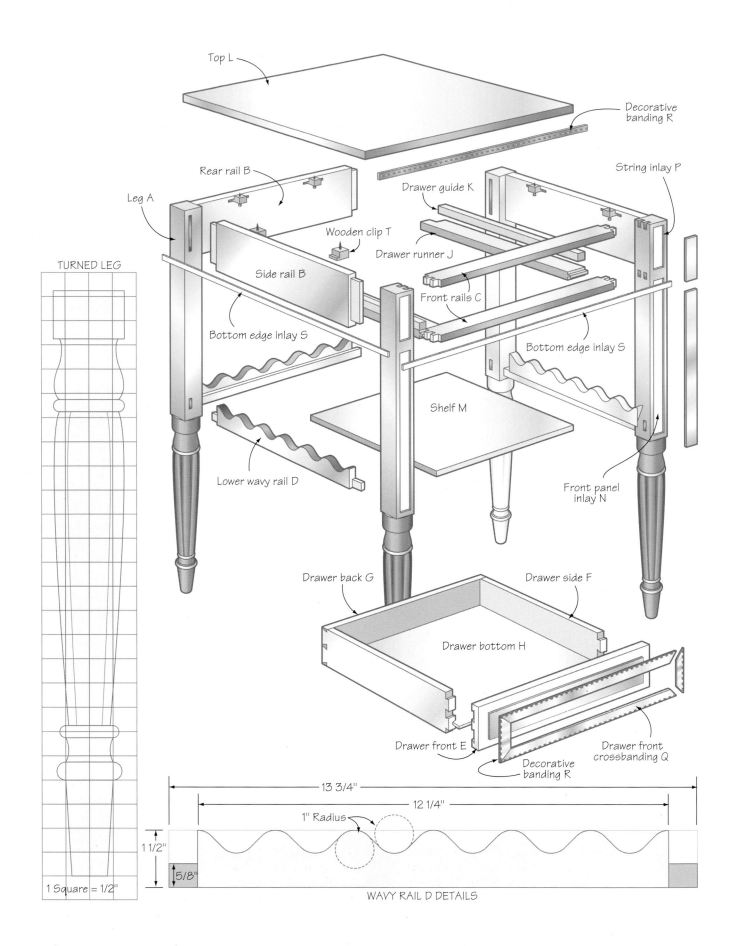

Top L

Decorative banding R

Rear rail B

Drawer guide K

String inlay P

Leg A

Wooden clip T

Side rail B

Drawer runner J

Front rails C

TURNED LEG

Bottom edge inlay S

Bottom edge inlay S

Shelf M

Lower wavy rail D

Front panel inlay N

Drawer back G

Drawer side F

Drawer bottom H

Drawer front E

Decorative banding R

Drawer front crossbanding Q

1 Square = 1/2"

13 3/4"

12 1/4"

1" Radius

1 1/2"

5/8"

WAVY RAIL D DETAILS

inches (millimeters)

REFERENCE	QUANTITY	PART	STOCK	THICKNESS	(mm)	WIDTH	(mm)	LENGTH	(mm)	COMMENTS
A	4	legs	mahogany	$1\frac{1}{2}$	(38)	$1\frac{1}{2}$	(38)	$27\frac{1}{8}$	(689)	
B	3	side and rear rails	mahogany	$\frac{3}{4}$	(19)	$4\frac{1}{4}$	(108)	$13\frac{3}{4}$	(349)	$\frac{3}{4}$" (19) TBE
C	2	front rails	mahogany	$\frac{5}{8}$	(16)	$1\frac{1}{2}$	(38)	$13\frac{3}{4}$	(349)	$\frac{3}{4}$" (19) TBE
D	4	lower wavy rails	mahogany	$\frac{1}{2}$	(13)	$1\frac{1}{2}$	(38)	$13\frac{3}{4}$	(349)	$\frac{3}{4}$" (19) TBE
E	1	drawer front	bird's-eye maple	$\frac{7}{8}$	(22)	3	(76)	$12\frac{3}{16}$	(310)	
F	2	drawer sides	pine	$\frac{7}{16}$	(11)	3	(76)	$13\frac{5}{8}$	(346)	
G	1	drawer back	pine	$\frac{7}{16}$	(11)	$2\frac{3}{8}$	(61)	$12\frac{3}{16}$	(310)	
H	1	drawer bottom	pine	$\frac{1}{2}$	(13)	$11\frac{3}{4}$	(298)	$13\frac{5}{8}$	(346)	
J	2	drawer runners	pine	$\frac{5}{8}$	(16)	$1\frac{5}{8}$	(41)	$13\frac{1}{4}$	(336)	$\frac{3}{8}$" (10) TOE
K	2	drawer guides	pine	$\frac{5}{8}$	(16)	$\frac{3}{4}$	(19)	$12\frac{1}{8}$	(308)	
L	1	top	mahogany	$\frac{3}{4}$	(19)	$16\frac{1}{2}$	(419)	$16\frac{3}{4}$	(425)	
M	1	shelf	mahogany	$\frac{1}{2}$	(13)	$14\frac{3}{4}$	(375)	$14\frac{3}{4}$	(375)	
N	1	front panel inlay	bird's-eye maple	$\frac{3}{4}$	(19)	4	(102)	24	(610)	4 inlay pieces from board
P		string inlay	ebony	$\frac{1}{8}$	(3)	$\frac{1}{8}$	(3)	7 lf	(2134)	
Q		drawer front crossbanding	mahogany	$\frac{3}{16}$	(5)	$\frac{3}{4}$	(19)	3 lf	(914)	
R		Rockler inlay (dec. banding)				$\frac{5}{16}$	(8)	5 lf	(1524)	drawer and top (Rockler item #18812)
S		front and sides bttm edge inlay	tiger maple	$\frac{3}{16}$	(5)	$\frac{1}{4}$	(6)	4 lf	(1219)	
T	4	wooden clips	pine	$\frac{1}{2}$	(13)	$\frac{7}{8}$	(22)	4	(102)	

Note: TBE = tenon both ends; TOE = tenon one end.

hardware

2	$1\frac{1}{2}$" (38mm) Antique-finish knobs with bolt fitting	item #H-46	Horton Brasses
	$1\frac{1}{2}$" (38mm) Clout nails		
	Cyanoacrylate glue		
	Oil/varnish mixture		
	Paste wax		

The jig used for beading or reeding

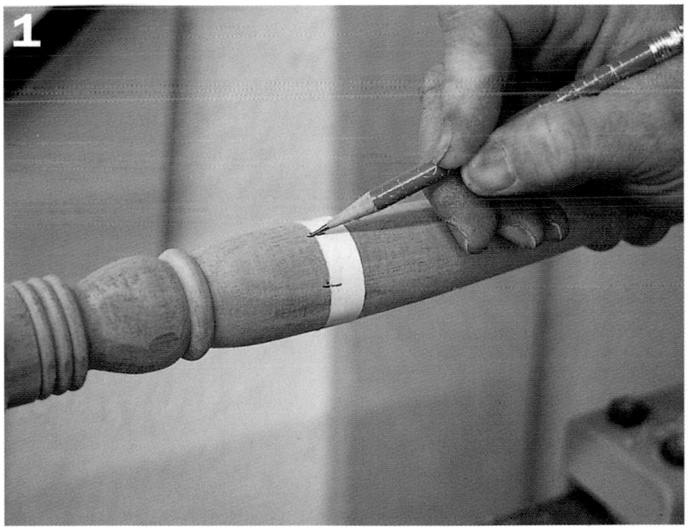

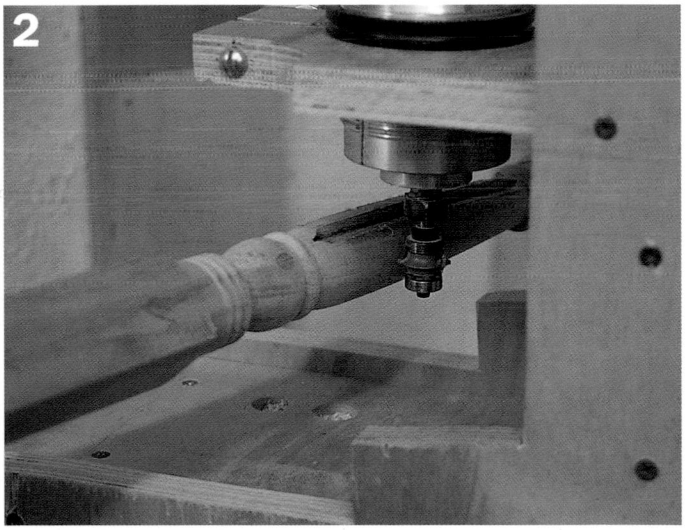

step 1 Begin by turning the lower portion of the legs according to the plan. To create the reeds, wrap a strip of paper around the turning at the largest diameter and mark the point where the paper overlaps. Remove the paper, trim to that mark, then lay out six equal spaces. Rewrap the paper in the same location and transfer the marks onto the turning. This is a simple method to divide a turning into equal sections.

step 2 The method that you use to cut the beads on this project depends on the lathe that you use. The jig I use is an L-shaped bracket that my trim router sets into. The bit is a Lee Valley beading bit. Adjust the point of the bit at the center of the turning or exactly at the center of the drive spur. Run the cut the length of the post, stopping before touching the bead at the top and bottom. From here, you will have to finish the carving by hand.

step 3 Mark and cut the mortises for all the rails. The front rail mortises are twin mortise and tenons (see step 6). You can also see the finished carving from the previous step.

step 4 Cut the tenons on the side and rear rails. (For more information, see project five, steps 7 through 8).

step 5 To create the twin tenon, make the shoulder cut on the ¾" sides only. Using a tenoning jig, make the edge cut for both edges and reset the jig to remove the waste between the tenons.

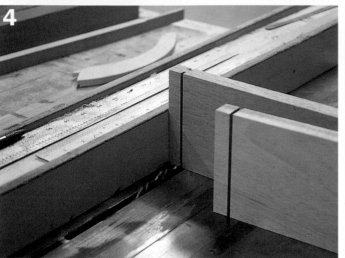

step 6 This is the finished twin mortise-and-tenon joint used for both front rails. Cut the mortises in the back edge of the bottom front rail to accept the drawer runner tenons.

step 7 For the wavy rails around the tray, begin with a ¼" cut on the face of the piece, then make a second cut on the opposite face with the fence set ½" away from the blade.

step 8 Reset the fence to ¼", then raise the blade to remove the ⅞" waste up to the second cut made. This produces an L-shaped profile.

step 9 Finally, make the cheek cut that leaves the necessary tenon.

step 10 Make a pattern of the wavy design with a piece of ½" plywood. Cut a groove into the plywood so that the stock snugly fits into the groove.

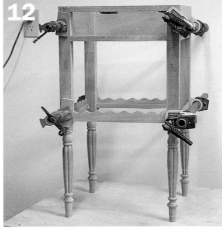

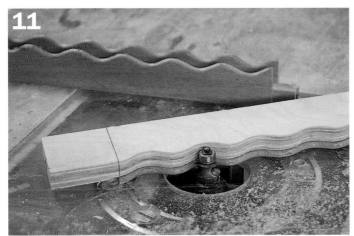

step 11 Fit the stock into the groove, with the ends of the stock located at the top of a wave, and with a ¼" beading bit set to the correct height, make the cut, creating the wavy design. You should make this a climb cut or move against the spin of the bit.

step 12 Assemble the table in steps. First, glue the side rails to the legs, then, when dry, glue the front and rear rails. Before you assemble the rear rail, cut the slots for the wood clips near the ends of the piece (see step 17).

step 13 Mill the shelf to size and make a ¼" × ¼" rabbet on all edges. Slide the piece into the area, allowing the front edge to rest against the back side of the front legs. Mark where the edge of the leg meets the shelf. Repeat this process on all four sides of the shelf. When complete, extend the marks to form the area that needs to be removed so that the shelf fits between the legs.

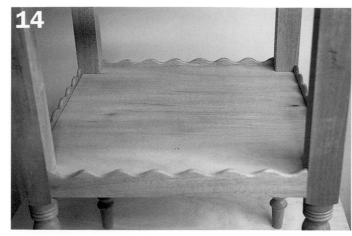

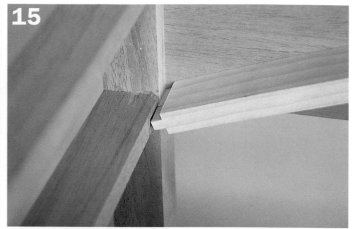

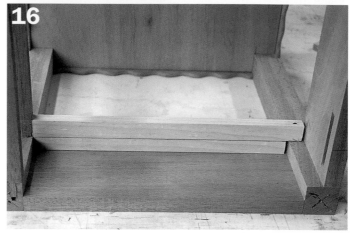

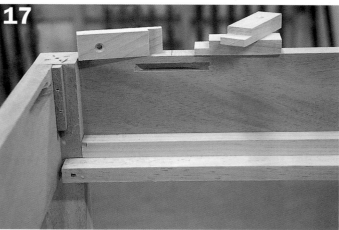

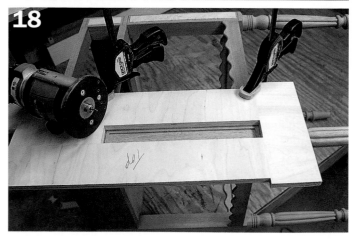

step 14 Make the cuts on the shelf and check the fit.

step 15 Prepare the drawer runners and guides and make the tenon on one end of each runner. Remove the tenon at the front leg and cut a notch at the rear leg.

step 16 Glue the mortise and tenon, slide the runner into place, hold tightly to the front rail and nail into the rear post to secure. Glue and nail the drawer guide into place, even with the two posts.

step 17 Use a biscuit joiner to cut the slots for the wooden clips. Set the cut to begin ¼" down from the top edge. Cut a ¼" slot. Make the wooden clips for the top. Secure with No 8 × 1" wood screws.

step 18 Make a jig for cutting the inlay by using ½" birch plywood and biscuit joinery. Remember to oversize the area to compensate for the inlay bushing. Mark the edges of the inlay jig carefully. Using the ⅛" bit, cut the leg for the inlay and remove the waste.

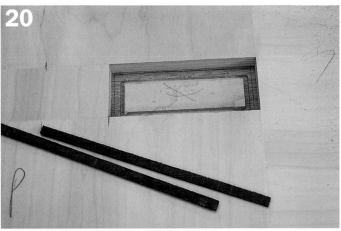

step 19 Following the directions with the inlay kit, cut the material for each of the front panel inlay areas and glue in place.

step 20 Place the jig back at the marks created in step 18. With the same setup, carefully cut a ⅛" groove around each inlay for the ebony string inlay. Mill the string inlay to size and glue. When dry, sand the inlay smooth.

step 21 Cut a ¼"-wide by ⅛"-deep groove on the front and both sides, even with the bottom edge of the rails. Cut an inlay of tiger maple to fill the groove and glue it in place, allowing the front to overlap the sides, hiding the ends of the inlay.

step 22 Build the drawer. Begin by laying out the dovetails on the drawer front. Cut the lines down to a line scribed ⁷⁄₁₆" from the inside of the drawer front. Overcut toward the center of the interior face of the front. A front this size has two full tails, one pin and two half pins.

step 23 With a Forstner bit, cut away some of the waste, then clean the area with your chisels.

step 24 Set the front onto a side piece with the inside even with a line scribed ⁷⁄₁₆" from the end of the side and mark with a sharp pencil. Remove the waste area with the chisel and test the fit.

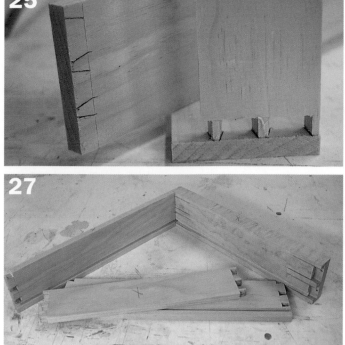

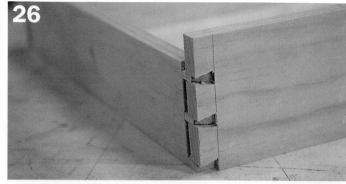

step 25 Lay out the back piece so there are two full pins and one half pin at the top. Cut those pins, removing the area of the tails. Set the back onto the side and transfer the marks from the back to the sides as shown. Then remove the waste, leaving the tails.

step 26 This is a look at how the side tails fit into the drawer back pins.

step 27 With the dovetails complete, cut a ¼" groove that is half the thickness of the drawer sides for the bottom.

step 28 Cut the drawer bottom to size so the grain runs across the drawer and bevel three edges — the two end-grain ends and one other edge — to fit the groove. Make a ⅛" cut into the drawer bottom, just to the inside edge of the back piece.

step 29 With the drawer apart, set the saw blade to ¾" and cut the front on all sides, creating the shoulder for the crossbanding.

step 30 Cut the crossbanding on the band saw, noticing the grain direction, and fit to the drawer front with mitered corners. Use cyanoacrylate glue to bond the banding to the drawer face.

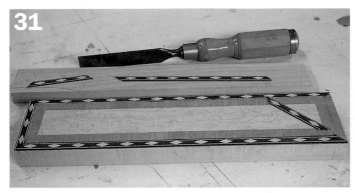

step 31 Repeat the process to install the decorative banding, as well.

step 32 With a $^5/_{16}$" straight-cut bit in the router table, run the front edge of the top, creating the groove for the decorative inlay. Glue the strip in place.

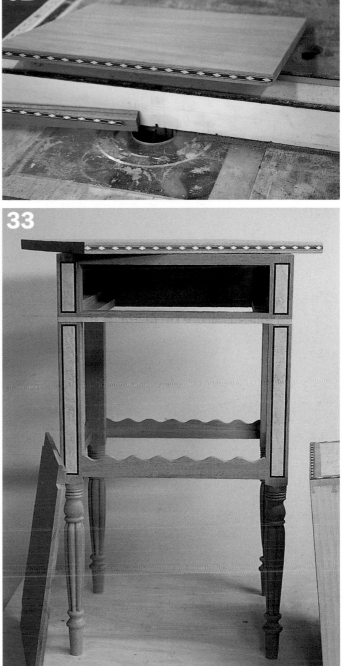

step 33 Sand the table completely, then you're ready to finish. The finish I use is an oil/varnish mixture. Three to four coats give a good sheen and protection. Then a coat of paste wax seals the deal.

step 34 Install the knobs by drilling the location with a $^3/_{32}$" bit through the front. On the inside of the drawer front, drill a $^5/_8$" hole $^1/_2$" deep with a Forstner bit to recess the nut on the inside. Compete the process by redrilling the first hole with a $^3/_{16}$" bit. Cut the knob shaft to size and attach the knob.

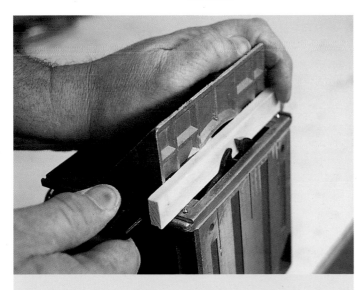

t i p | To set the depth of the biscuit joiner, cut a scrap to the thickness necessary, set the piece against the blade that is extended, then bring the fence tight to that scrap. Make sure the tool is unplugged!

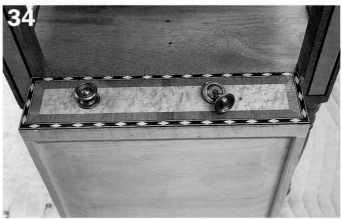

MARBLE-TOP ART DECO TABLE

Created in the likeness of a piece designed by French designer Maurice Dufrene in the 1930s, this round Art Deco side table has it all. A marble slab is inset into a bold, round top, a strong center column creates shadows in the light and an understated ring shaped base is slightly elevated.

The top is created much like a wagon wheel, using segments to produce the circular element. Other parts are turned on the lathe, and the column has a straightforward design that shouts Art Deco.

If you are a student of this style of furniture, you will absolutely have to build this table.

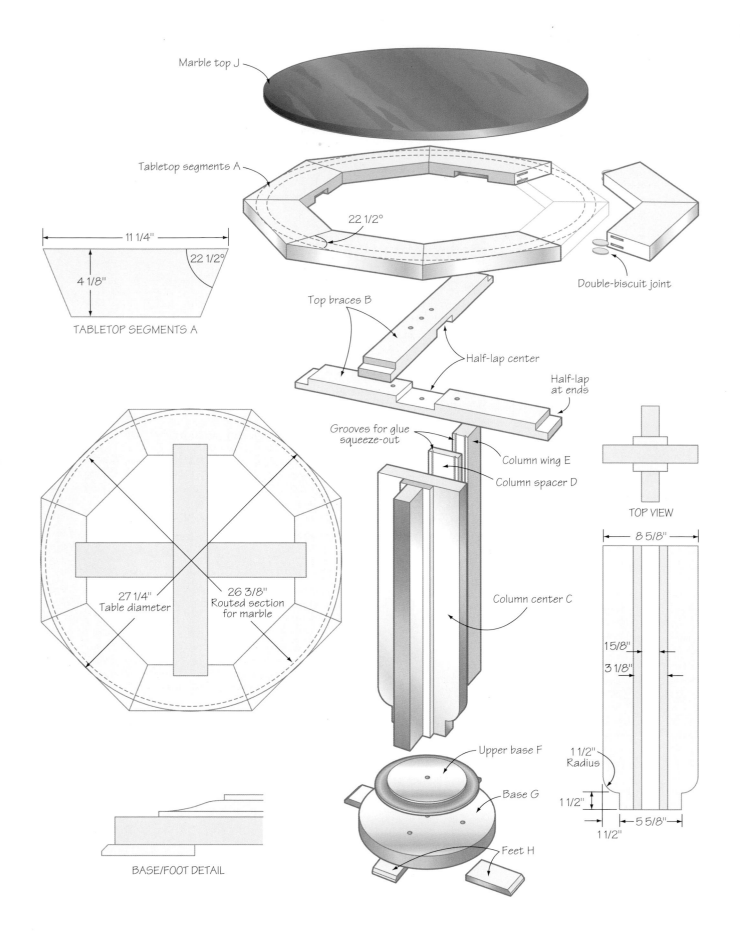

Marble top J

Tabletop segments A

22 1/2°

11 1/4"

22 1/2°

4 1/8"

TABLETOP SEGMENTS A

Double-biscuit joint

Top braces B

Half-lap center

Half-lap
at ends

Grooves for glue
squeeze-out

Column wing E

Column spacer D

27 1/4"
Table diameter

26 3/8"
Routed section
for marble

Column center C

TOP VIEW

8 5/8"

15/8"

3 1/8"

1 1/2"
Radius

1 1/2"

5 5/8"

1 1/2"

Upper base F

Base G

Feet H

BASE/FOOT DETAIL

inches (millimeters)

REFERENCE	QUANTITY	PART	STOCK	THICKNESS	(mm)	WIDTH	(mm)	LENGTH	(mm)	COMMENTS
A	8	tabletop segments	mahogany	$1^3/_4$	(45)	$4^1/_4$	(108)	$11^1/_4$	(285)	$22^1/_2°$ cut BE
B	2	top braces	mahogany	$1^1/_2$	(38)	$3^1/_8$	(79)	$20^7/_8$	(530)	$^1/_2$" (13) lapped center
C	1	column center	mahogany	$1^5/_8$	(41)	$8^5/_8$	(219)	$23^3/_4$	(603)	
D	2	column spacers	mahogany	$^3/_4$	(19)	$3^1/_8$	(79)	$23^3/_4$	(603)	
E	2	column wings	mahogany	$1^3/_4$	(45)	$2^3/_4$	(70)	$23^3/_4$	(603)	
F	1	upper base	mahogany	1	(25)	$9^5/_8$	(245)	$9^5/_8$	(245)	lathe-turned
G	1	base	mahogany	$1^1/_4$	(32)	$13^5/_8$	(346)	$13^5/_8$	(346)	lathe-turned
H	4	feet	mahogany	$^1/_2$	(13)	$1^5/_8$	(41)	$4^1/_4$	(108)	
J	1	top	marble	$^3/_4$	(19)	$26^3/_8$	(670)	round		

Note: BE = both ends.

hardware

8	No. 8 x $1^1/_4$" (32mm) Slotted-head wood screws		local hardware store
5	No. 8 x 2" (51mm) Square-drive deck screws		local hardware store
5	$^5/_{16}$" x 4" (8mm x 102mm) Lag screw with washers		local hardware store
12	No. 7 x $^3/_4$" (19mm) Slotted-head wood screws		local hardware store
	Glue		
	#20 Biscuits		
	$^3/_{16}$" (5mm) Dowel pin		
	$^1/_4$" (6mm) Spacer		
	$^3/_{16}$" × 1" (5mm × 25mm) Dowel		
	Aniline dye stain		
	Lacquer, sealer and finish		

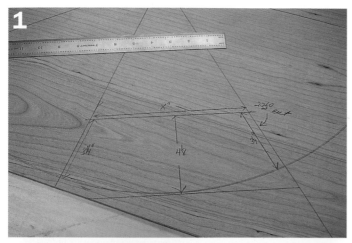

step 1 To start this piece, you need to determine the size of the segmented top. Create a full-size drawing of the round top and divide the circumference into eight sections. The eight sections determine the 22½° cut for each end of the sections. Lay back 3¼" from the intersection of the circle and the section dividing line to ensure space for the biscuit joinery. From that back line, measure out to just past the apex of the circle. To copy my piece, the result is a 4¼"-wide piece that is 11¼" on the long side.

step 2 Mill your segment pieces to size and cut the 22½° cuts on each end to form a pie-shaped piece. Repeat the cuts on all eight pieces.

step 3 Clamp the pieces with a band clamp. If your measurements were correct, the fit is tight. If you are off a bit, you can make small changes to the angle cuts on individual pieces to arrive at a tight fit. When ready, mark the location for the biscuit slot.

step 4 On the segments, transfer the layout line for the biscuit slots to both faces of the piece and cut one slot referenced to the top and one to the bottom, creating twin slots on each end.

step 5 Glue the ends with the biscuits in place and clamp with a band clamp until dry.

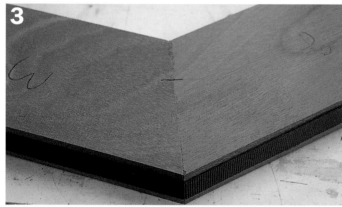

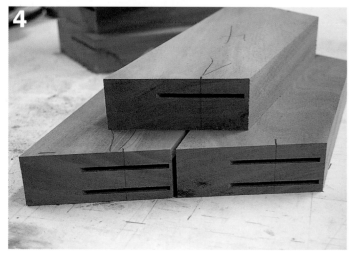

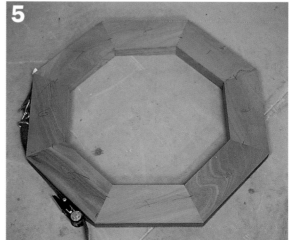

step 6 Cut the top braces to size and create the half-lap center joint.

step 7 Assemble the top braces and mark all four ends with an X. Separate the two and cut a $3/4" \times 1"$ rabbet on the ends of each brace. Cut only the X-marked ends, so that when joined the braces have the cuts on the same face.

step 8 Set the brace assembly in place on the underside of the joined top and mark the ends. Remove the necessary areas with a router or chisels. It helps to keep the brace in the same position to match the cuts, so mark one end with the top section location.

step 9 Before you attach the brace assembly to the top, locate a center in the brace and drill a $3/16"$ hole. Secure the brace with glue and $1 1/4"$ screws in the center, then attach the assembly to the top in the same manner.

step 10 Prepare your band saw to cut the top section to round. Attach a cleat that fits into the saw guide to a piece of plywood. Square a line from the blade and mark $13 1/8"$, or half the diameter of the finished top. Drill a $3/16"$ hole for a short dowel pin.

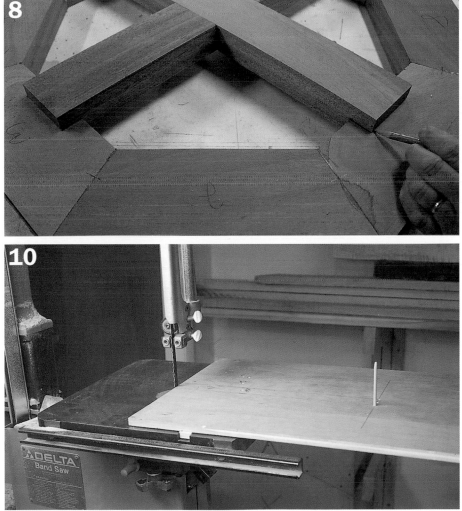

step 11 Place the top section onto the pin in the plywood platform with a flat area at the blade. It will be a tight fit. Turn the saw on and slowly rotate the top section, cutting to a circle.

step 12 Once cut, sand all surfaces of the now round top. Round over both the top and bottom exterior edges with a $^3/_{16}$" roundover bit.

step 13 Set up the plunge router with the circle-cutting jig. Place the $^3/_{16}$" dowel pin in place, then add a $^1/_4$" spacer to the pin. Set the router to cut $^1/_4$" deep, and the outside cutting edge of the bit ($^3/_4$" straight) to be exactly $^5/_{16}$" from the outside edge of the top. Hook the circle-cutting jig over the pin and plunge-cut the first pass on the top. With the outer edge defined, move to the extreme inside cut and repeat the process, each time moving toward the outer edge. This process allows the router base to rest on the existing material with each pass, and on the top's outer rim on the final passing cut. Also, notice how I lock the top in place with the plywood pieces. It will need to be secured.

step 14 When the cutting is complete, clean up the recessed top with a scraper.

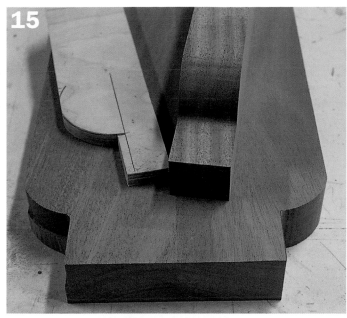

step 15 Next, mill the pieces for the column. Make the 1½"-radius cut at both edges of the column center and one edge of each of the column wings. It is easy to create a simple jig and use a router and pattern bit to complete this step.

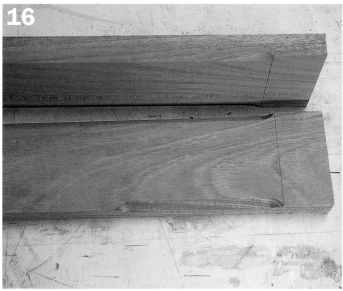

step 16 Use a chamfer bit and router on both edges of the two column spacers. Stay short of the ends for appearance.

step 17 At the table saw, cut a shallow groove on the back sides of the spacers and wings. Make the cut on both edges. This will become a reservoir to prevent glue squeeze-out during the assembly of the column.

step 18 Attach the wings to the center of the spacers with glue and 1¼" screws. Use just enough glue to work; a slight excess should be caught in the grooves from the previous step, but too much will still result in squeeze-out.

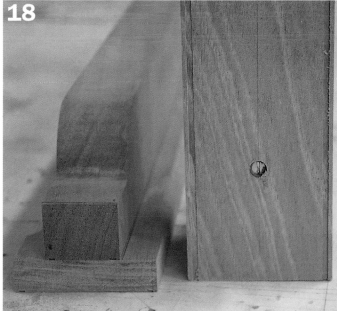

step 19 This is how the wing/spacer unit attaches to the column center. Because we are joining face grain, the connection is made with glue only.

step 20 Make the connection in two steps: one side, then the other when the first is dry.

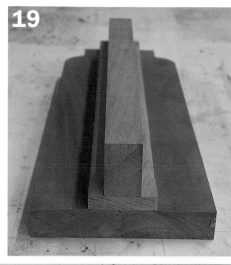

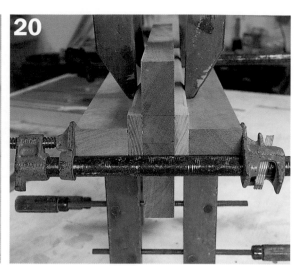

step 21 Mill and turn the upper base to profile and the base to size. With the base on the lathe, mark the exact center. Drill a $^{3}/_{16}$" hole at center of the base and at the intersection of the lines used to mount the face plate onto the upper base (this is the bottom side).

step 22 Insert a short dowel into the base and slide the upper base onto the pin. Mark a line around the upper base onto the base. Remount the base on the lathe and cut a shallow groove just inside the marked line. This is another glue reservoir.

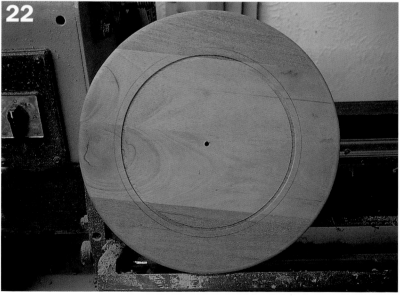

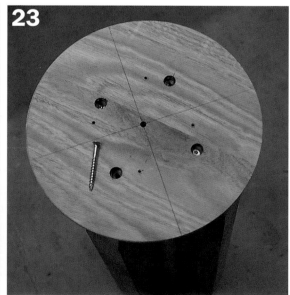

step 23 Attach the upper base to the column with 2" screws, making sure the heads are countersunk.

step 24 Spread glue onto the bottom side of the upper base and inside the groove cut into the top of the base. Using the dowel pin, attach the two and clamp until dry.

step 25 Mill the feet to size, cut a chamfer on the ends, then cut the blank into two equal pieces. Locate the feet directly in alignment with the column edges and attach with glue and $^3/_4$" screws. Countersink the heads.

step 26 Predrill the top and column for the $^5/_{16}$" lag screws. Drill a $^7/_8$" countersunk hole in the top so that the washer and the lag-screw head will be recessed. Finish the hole with a $^5/_{16}$" bit. Set the top in place on the legs and mark the hole locations. Predrill the column with a $^1/_4$" bit. Attach the top to the column with the lag screws.

step 27 The finish I selected for this piece is a water-based aniline dye stain with a lacquer top coat. All that is left is to order the marble insert for the top and set it in place to finish the project.

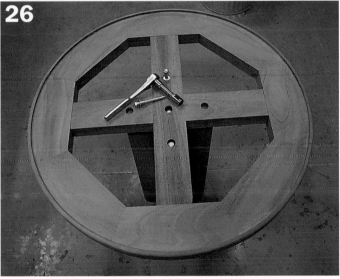

tip | Here's a hint: If the marble proves to be a bit too costly, contact a kitchen countertop manufacturer for a solid-surface tabletop. These products will also work nicely and come in some great new colors and designs.

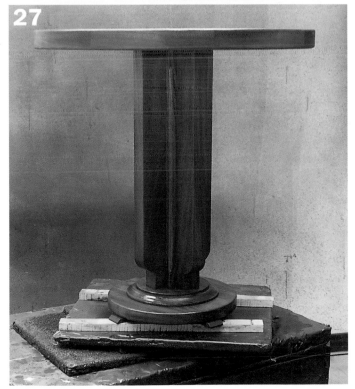

CD CABINET

In my book *Fine Furniture for a Lifetime*, one of the projects was a reproduction of a Federal-period sideboard with tambour doors of alternating hardwood. Since that time I have thought of incorporating that same 1790s idea into a cabinet of contemporary design.

The sweeping curves of the laminated sides and slight bow of the front of this design draw your eyes inward to the tambour doors. The pairing of tiger maple and bubinga makes the piece pop, and upon opening the case you are surprised by the boldness of the bubinga interior.

And, hey, there are also a few compartments to show off your favorite things.

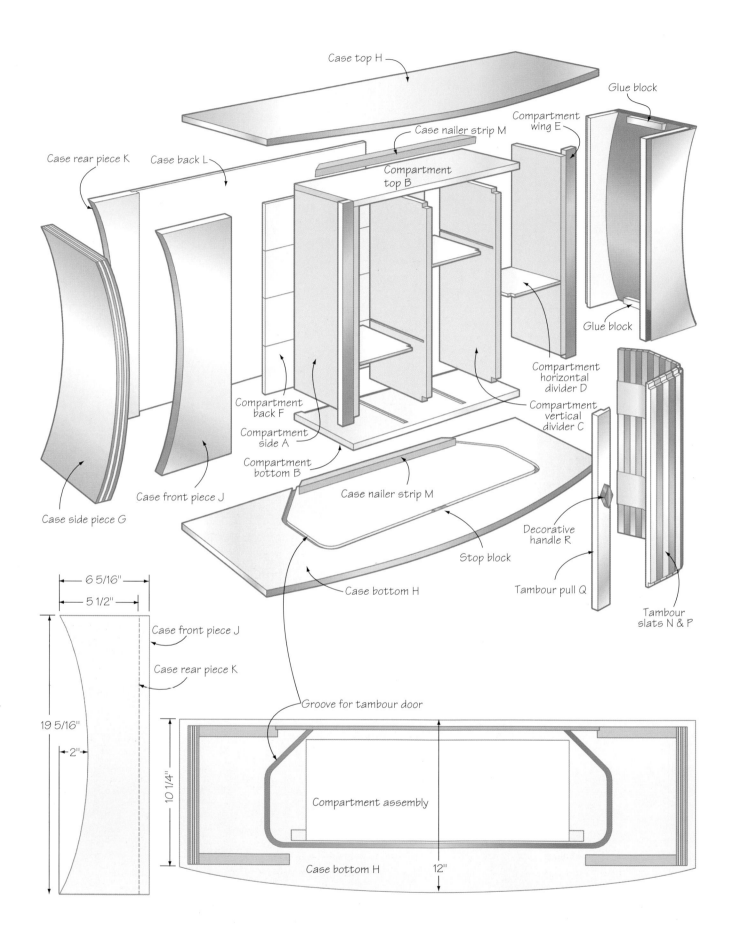

Case top H

Glue block

Compartment
wing E

Case nailer strip M

Case rear piece K

Case back L

Compartment
top B

Glue block

Compartment
horizontal
divider D

Compartment
back F

Compartment
vertical
divider C

Compartment
side A

Case front piece J

Compartment
bottom B

Case side piece G

Case nailer strip M

Decorative
handle R

Stop block

Case bottom H

Tambour pull Q

Tambour
slats N & P

6 5/16"

5 1/2"

Case front piece J

Case rear piece K

19 5/16"

2"

Groove for tambour door

10 1/4"

Compartment assembly

Case bottom H

12"

CD CABINET

inches (millimeters)

REFERENCE	QUANTITY	PART	STOCK	THICKNESS	(mm)	WIDTH	(mm)	LENGTH	(mm)	COMMENTS
A	2	compartment sides	bubinga	$3/4$	(19)	7	(178)	18	(457)	
B	2	compartment top and bottom	bubinga	$3/4$	(19)	7	(178)	$18^{1}/4$	(463)	
C	2	compartment vertical dividers	bubinga	$1/2$	(13)	$6^{5}/8$	(168)	$18^{3}/8$	(467)	
D	3	compartment horizontal dividers	bubinga	$1/4$	(6)	$6^{5}/8$	(168)	$5^{5}/8$	(143)	
E	2	compartment wing pieces	bubinga	$3/4$	(19)	1	(25)	$19^{1}/4$	(489)	
F	1	compartment back	tiger maple	$5/16$	(8)	$17^{5}/16$	(440)	$18^{9}/16$	(471)	many pieces
G	10	case sides	tiger maple	$5/32$	(4)	10	(254)	24	(610)	
H	2	case top and bottom	tiger maple	$3/4$	(19)	12	(305)	$35^{3}/4$	(908)	
J	2	case front pieces	tiger maple	$3/4$	(19)	$6^{5}/16$	(160)	$19^{5}/16$	(491)	
K	2	case rear pieces	tiger maple	$3/4$	(19)	$4^{1}/2$	(115)	$19^{5}/16$	(491)	
L	1	case back	plywood	$1/4$	(6)	$22^{7}/16$	(570)	$19^{5}/16$	(491)	
M	2	case nailer strips	poplar	$3/4$	(19)	1	(25)	$20^{1}/2$	(521)	
N	17	tambour slats	tiger maple	$1/2$	(13)	$5/8$	(16)	21	(533)	
P	17	tambour slats	bubinga	$1/2$	(13)	$5/8$	(16)	21	(533)	
Q	2	tambour pulls		$3/4$	(19)	$1^{1}/8$	(28)	19	(483)	one of each hardwood
R	2	decorative handles	ebony	$3/8$	(10)	$1/2$	(13)	2	(51)	

hardware

3 pairs	CD holders		item #92908	Rockler
1	$3/16$" (5mm) Brass rod	.		local hardware store
	Screws			
	Glue			
	Glue blocks			
	Canvas			
	Wax			
	$3/4$" (19mm) Flathead wood screws			
	Small stop			
	Oil/varnish mixture			
	Brad nails			
	Epoxy			

step 1 Begin this piece by milling to size the compartment sides, top and bottom. Lay out the $1/2$" dadoes for the vertical dividers in the top and bottom, and using a simple jig or straightedge and a pattern bit, cut the dadoes, stopping just short of the piece's front edge.

step 2 Next, switch to a $1/4$" straight bit and cut the sides for the horizontal dividers. To make a straightedge jig without having a pattern bit, see project 11, step 5.

step 3 Grab the router with a rabbet bit and create the rabbets for the compartment back. Cut from end to end on the rear edge of the sides while stopping just short of the ends of the top and bottom pieces.

step 4 Attach the four pieces forming the interior box. Countersink the screw heads.

step 5 Mill the vertical dividers to size, lay out the dadoes for the horizontal dividers, matching the dadoes already in the side pieces, and notch the front edges so that the dividers slip over the stop-dado in the top and bottom to align with the front edge of the box. Repeat the same process for the horizontal dividers.

step 6 Before you install the horizontal dividers, attach the compartment wing pieces to the front edge of the box sides by simply gluing. Also, mill the compartment back pieces with shiplapped edges.

step 7 Cut the pieces for the case sides, apply the glue and clamp them in the form until dry. See the sidebar at the end of the project for building a bending form.

step 8 Clean the excess glue from the edges, run one edge over the jointer and cut the sides to width. Using a pair of squares and a ruler, mark the middle of one of the laminated sides. Set a scrap piece cut to the length of the sides (19$\frac{5}{16}$") with the exact middle marked in place so that the marks line up. Transfer the locations of the top and bottom cuts from the scrap onto the sides.

step 9 With one side marked, align the other side to the first and mark the top and bottom cuts, as well as the center mark. This corrects any slight variation in the sides.

step 10 Clamp the scrap to the sides, aligning the three marks as shown, and make the cut for the top and bottom of both sides. You will need to elevate the pieces to accommodate the curve of the ends.

step 11 Next, glue the case front pieces to the sides so that the ends of the front piece are flush at the corners of the side.

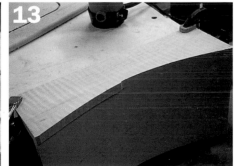

step 12 When dry, tip the blade to 45° and make the decorative cut into the exterior edge of the front pieces.

step 13 Cut away a majority of the excess front and use a flush-trim bit with a bottom-mounted bearing to trim.

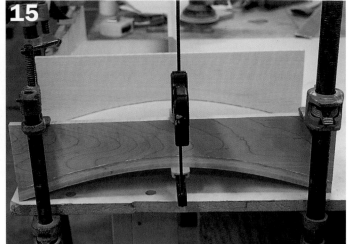

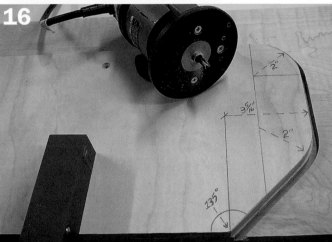

step 14 Use the case side to mark the bend onto the case rear pieces. Cut and smooth the arc, making sure to orient the top, bottom and the matching side. Then cut a ⅜" × ¼" rabbet for the case back on the inside edge of the rear pieces.

step 15 Glue and clamp the rear pieces to the case sides as shown.

step 16 Mill the case top and bottom to size and lay out a template of the track for the tambour doors. Route a ⁵⁄₁₆" groove in both the top and bottom pieces. These must be mirror images of one another. To assure this, mark the center of your template and the centers of the pieces, and align before routing. The router bushing rides against the template.

step 17 Use a pipe clamp and a thin piece of stock to create the gentle bow in the top and bottom of the case. Cut and smooth the bottom, then align the top and use the bottom as a guide to rout the top to an identical bow.

step 18 Use a ¼" roundover bit on both surfaces of the pieces. Run the front and sides.

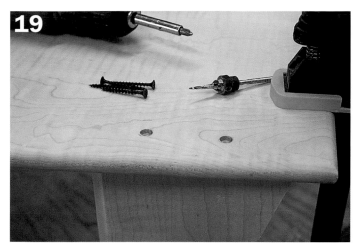

step 19 Sand all the pieces completely and attach the sides to the top and bottom with screws into the case front and rear pieces. Add glue blocks to the inside of each side at the center, top and bottom. They will be slightly angled to fit against the laminated sides.

step 20 Cut the slats for the tambour doors, making sure that they are straight. Lay them out in alternating hardwood. On a piece of melamine, place two strips of canvas as shown. Apply the glue to the canvas with a brush, enough to glue the pieces to the canvas but not so much as to squeeze between the slats. Work quickly, a few inches at a time. When complete, use clamps to tightly pull the slats to the straightedge. Slide a second piece of melamine over the glued door slats, apply clamps to secure and let dry. You can do this in one step, then cut the tambour into two equal pieces, or repeat the process two times — one for each door.

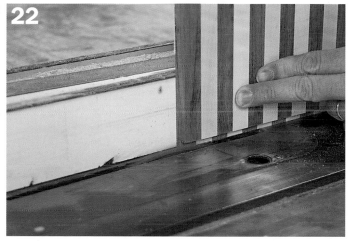

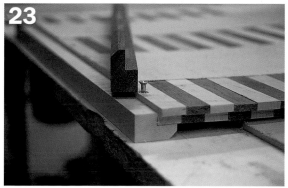

step 21 Square one end of the panels, then trim to the final size.

step 22 Create a rabbet on the front side of the door panels, leaving the size needed to slide in the grooves at the top and bottom ($\frac{1}{4}$"). Make the cut and try the panel. A second trimming may be necessary. You want the sliding to be almost effortless. Wax the groove to aid in the travel.

step 23 Mill the tambour pulls by beveling the outer edge and cutting a $\frac{3}{8}$" × $\frac{1}{4}$" rabbet in the back edge. Predrill through the slats and attach the panel to the pulls with a $\frac{3}{4}$" flathead wood screw. These will need to be detached and reassembled a few times, so don't add glue.

24

25

26

step 24 Slide the door panels into the case and attach the pulls again. Make any adjustments to the fit of the pulls. They should meet together nicely. When you are satisfied with the fit, push the panels together and mark the location for a small stop that will be glued into the track.

step 25 Cut the nailer strips to fit. Here you can see that the plywood back is to slide in front of the rear pieces and is attached to the nailer, thus hiding the raw edge of the plywood.

step 26 Apply your finish — I used multiple coats of an oil/ varnish mixture — then install the CD racks. Nail the back of the compartment into place to complete the compartment.

27

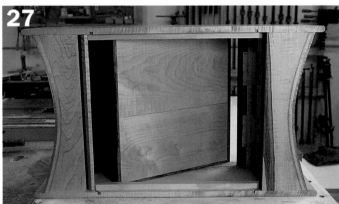

28

29

step 27 Install the doors and attach the pulls, then slide the compartment into the case from the front. Affix the compartment to the case bottom with four screws, countersink the heads and plug the holes.

step 28 The decorative ebony handles consist of two diamonds of ebony, four $\frac{3}{4}$" pieces of $\frac{3}{16}$" brass rod and two shorter pieces of rod. Make the handles and sand smooth, then drill two $\frac{3}{16}$" holes into the back of each handle.

step 29 Insert the shorter pieces of rod into the handle, coat the exposed end of the rod with a white grease pencil, place the piece onto the door pull and tap so that the rod end marks the location to drill. Drill the corresponding holes and affix the $\frac{3}{4}$" rods into both the handle and pull with epoxy. I use a scrap piece to ensure that the handles will be lined up.

creating a bending form

Another option for creating a bending form can be found in the sidebar at the end of project nine.

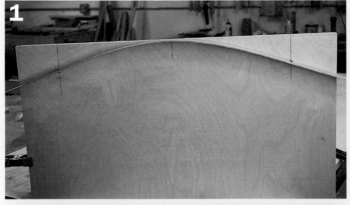

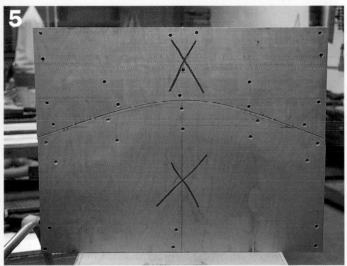

step 1 Begin your form with a piece of birch plywood. Lay out the bend with a thin scrap of wood. I used $2\frac{1}{2}$" bend over the $19\frac{5}{16}$" length for the CD cabinet. Mark the bow, cut on the band saw, and sand or file smooth.

step 2 Make a second side using the first side as a pattern. Two identical sides are the result.

step 3 Attach a short section of 2×4 cut to the correct length to the sides. Use the pieces with the flat edge along the bend, as well as a few in the rear for support and clamping strength.

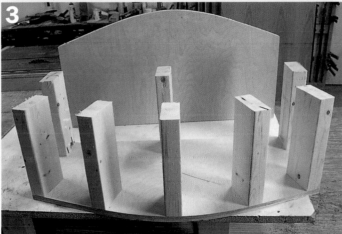

step 4 With the unit assembled, bend a piece of $\frac{1}{4}$" plywood over the form and attach it to the 2×4 edges with nails, placing screws at the two ends.

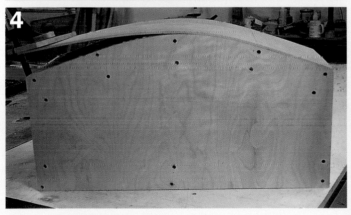

step 5 Use the first form to mark the sides for the opposing form. Repeat the same steps to complete the second form. You are now ready to laminate your pieces.

SLAT-BACK SIDE CHAIR

This chair design is a great first attempt. The innovative idea of the two-piece front legs allows the rails to join without the use of angled tenons, which can create many concerns for the beginning cabinetmaker.

Laminating the back legs creates the appropriate bend to provide support for the chair, as well as a strong connection to the seat area.

Add the contrasting color of the splines in the seat rails, the back slats and the simple inlay in the headrest, and the result not only pleases the eye, but will withstand many nights of stimulating conversation around the table.

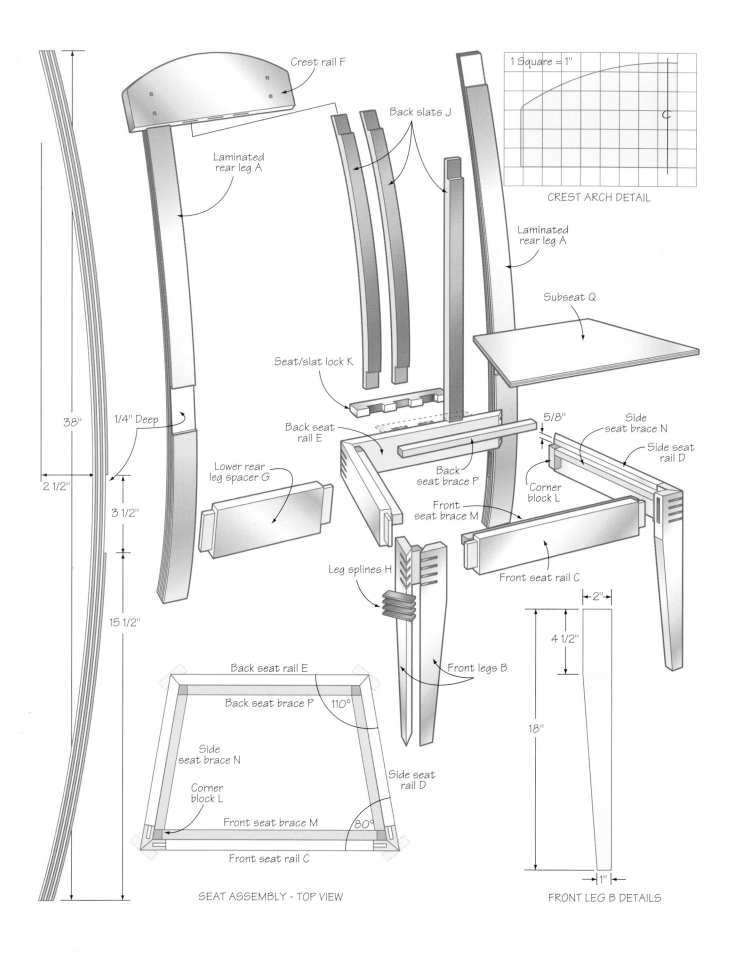

Crest rail F

Back slats J

1 Square = 1"

CREST ARCH DETAIL

C

Laminated
rear leg A

Laminated
rear leg A

Subseat Q

Seat/slat lock K

38"

1/4" Deep

Back seat
rail E

5/8"

Side
seat brace N

Side seat
rail D

2 1/2"

Lower rear
leg spacer G

Back
seat brace P

Corner
block L

3 1/2"

Front
seat brace M

Front seat rail C

15 1/2"

Leg splines H

Front legs B

2"

4 1/2"

Back seat rail E

Back seat brace P

110°

18"

Side
seat brace N

Corner
block L

Front seat brace M

80°

Side seat
rail D

SEAT ASSEMBLY - TOP VIEW

Front seat rail C

1"

FRONT LEG B DETAILS

inches (millimeters)

REFERENCE	QUANTITY	PART	STOCK	THICKNESS	(mm)	WIDTH	(mm)	LENGTH	(mm)	COMMENTS
A	6	laminated rear legs	tiger maple	1/4	(6)	4 1/2	(115)	42	(1067)	makes 2 rear legs
B	4	front legs	tiger maple	13/16	(21)	2	(51)	18	(457)	makes 2 front legs
C	1	front seat rail	tiger maple	13/16	(21)	3 1/2	(89)	18	(457)	1" (25) TBE
D	2	side seat rails	tiger maple	13/16	(21)	3 1/2	(89)	16	(406)	1" (25) TOE, 40° OE
E	1	back seat rail	tiger maple	13/16	(21)	3 1/2	(89)	16	(406)	40° cut BE
F	1	crest rail	tiger maple	3/4	(19)	5 1/2	(140)	15 1/4	(387)	arch is 13 1/2" (343) radius
G	1	lower rear leg spacer	tiger maple	3/4	(19)	3 1/2	(89)	10 1/2	(267)	1" (25) TBE
H	16	leg splines	walnut	1/8	(3)	3/4	(19)	2 1/4	(57)	
J	3	back slats	walnut	7/16	(11)	1 3/8	(35)	20	(508)	
K	1	seat/slat lock	tiger maple	3/4	(19)	1	(25)	8 1/4	(209)	
L	4	corner blocks	poplar	3/4	(19)	3/4	(19)	2 1/4	(57)	
M	1	front seat brace	poplar	3/4	(19)	3/4	(19)	16 3/8	(416)	
N	2	side seat braces	poplar	3/4	(19)	3/4	(19)	10 1/2	(267)	
P	1	back seat brace	poplar	3/4	(19)	3/4	(19)	12 1/2	(318)	
Q	1	subseat	Baltic birch ply	1/2	(13)	11 7/8	(301)	18	(457)	cut to fit

Note: TBE = tenon both ends; TOE = tenon one end; OE = one end; BE = both ends.

hardware

Glue

No. 8 × 1 1/4" (32mm) Wood screws

3/8" (10mm) Square plugs

Cyanoacrylate glue

Oil

Shellac

Dull-rubbed-effect lacquer (any low-sheen lacquer will work)

Upholstery materials or cushion

[handwritten note: note - this is what the fellow at Patricia's are centre was building small step stool]

step 1 Begin this piece by milling the pieces for the laminated legs, then bending them in the form until dry (see the sidebar "Creating a Bending Form" at the end of this project). When the pieces have been released from the form, clean one side on the jointer, keeping the face firmly against the fence, and rip it into two 2" legs.

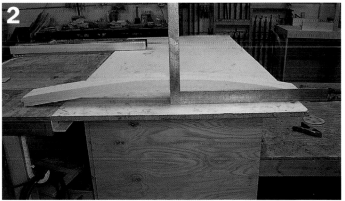

step 2 Locate the area for the back seat rail, then mark the top and bottom of the rail. Next, measure from the top edge of the back seat rail down 18", which is the floor line, and make a mark.

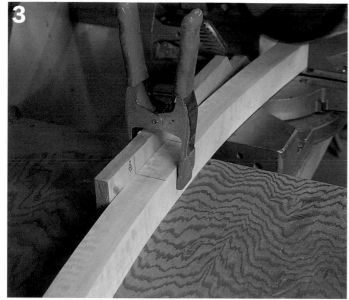

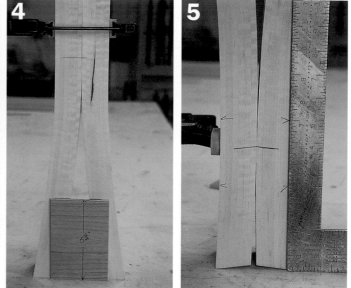

step 3 Holding the leg against the fence at the seat rail location, make a 90° cut at the floor line.

step 4 Clamp the legs together at the seat rail, while standing them on the floor cuts, and with a scrap that is 5½" tall, make a mark across the legs. At the same time, mark the height of the legs at 38" and cut the top of the leg as we did the floor line.

step 5 Set the clamp at the 5½" lines and clamp exactly at the line. Then mark the legs for the lower rear leg spacer mortises at both top and bottom. Connect the lines before removing the clamp. The spacer is 3½" wide and the mortise is 3".

step 6 Position the leg into the mortiser and adjust the position until the lines are perpendicular to the fence of the mortiser.

step 7 When set, cut the mortises for the rear leg spacer.

step 8 Next, move to the table saw and set the chair seat rail area on the back legs facedown on the saw. Maneuver the leg until the rail area is flat on the table, and clamp at each end. Raise the blade to cut $\frac{1}{4}$" and remove the waste, creating the recess for the back seat rail.

step 9 Repeat the same setup for the cut to determine the location of the crest rail. Then raise the blade to cut $\frac{1}{2}$" into the leg.

step 10 Use a tenoning jig to cut the area away for the crest rail. Remember to space the leg so that the top cut is flat on the table.

step 11 Cut and fit the lower rear leg spacer by creating the tenons that match the mortises in the leg.

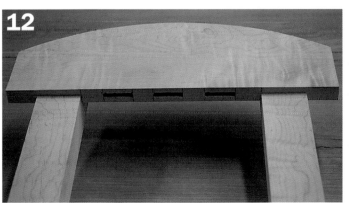

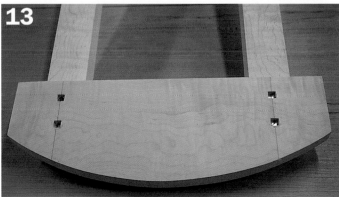

step 12 Cut the crest rail to size. Lay out for the $8\frac{1}{2}$" inside space equal to the lower spacer and mark the locations of the mortises for the back slats. Cut the $\frac{1}{4}$" mortises, then cut the arc in the top of the crest rail and sand smooth.

step 13 On the crest rail, lay out the location of the screws used to attach the rail to the legs. Use the $\frac{3}{8}$" mortising chisel to make a cut $\frac{1}{4}$" deep at the four locations. Screw the rail onto the legs, then plug the holes with a $\frac{3}{8}$" square plug and sand smooth.

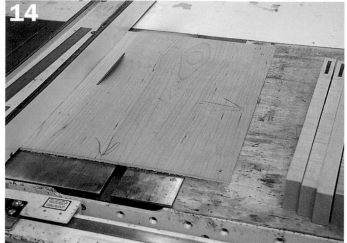

step 14 Prepare the pieces for the front legs of the chair, and cut the mortises for the front and side seat rails. Set the blade to 40° and raise the blade through a piece of $\frac{1}{4}$" plywood.

step 15 Move the fence close enough to the blade to cut a sharp edge on the legs. Run the legs through the saw with the face toward the fence, two legs with the mortise leading into the blade and two legs with the mortise on the other end. This will create two sets of leg pieces.

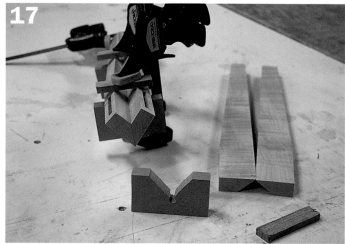

step 16 Lay out the cut to taper the legs. Start $4\frac{1}{2}$" down the leg and taper to 1" at the floor. I find that it is easy to mark the taper, cut it at the band saw just proud of the line and take a light cut with a pass over the jointer.

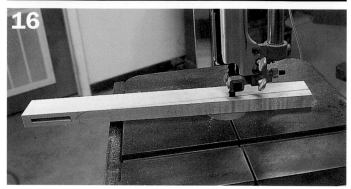

step 17 Glue the legs. Make these clamp pieces from scrap. I used medium-density fiberboard (MDF). The angle is 80°, and I simply drill a $\frac{1}{4}$" hole at the center of the layout and make the cuts at the band saw. The foot of the front leg will clamp easily, and this fixture, with a small piece bridging the legs, will put good pressure on the pieces.

step 18 While the glue is drying on the front legs, cut and prepare the rails for the seat assembly. Make the tenons on both ends of the front and one end of each side rail. Slide the tenons into the legs and set the unit on the worktable as shown. With a square set against the front rail, mark each side rail at $13\frac{1}{2}$".

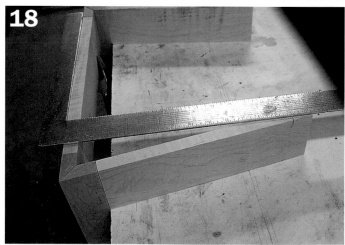

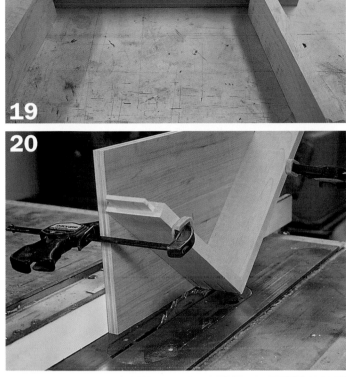

step 19 With the interior face flat on the bed, cut to the line with the angle set at 40°. Reassemble the pieces, then cut one end of the back rail at the same angle. With the points of the cuts aligned, mark the point and make the last cut on the back rail.

step 20 Glue the front legs and front rail and allow to dry. Use cyanoacrylate glue to join the side rails to the back rail. Attach the assembly to a piece of plywood so that the joint line is at a right angle to the table. Raise the blade to ³⁄₄" and make four passes over the blade, creating the leg spline areas. Repeat the process for both joints.

step 21 Cut the leg splines and glue them in place. Sand the joint flush.

step 22 Complete the same steps for the front leg assembly.

step 23 Finish the assembly of the seat section and attach with screws to the back legs.

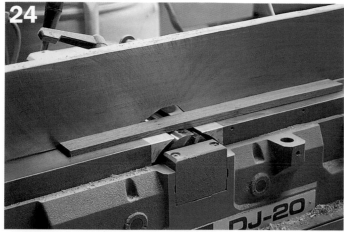

step 24 Prepare the stock for the back slats. Create a taper on each slat by setting the jointer cut at heavy $^3/_{32}$" and running the slat into the cut 7".

step 25 Flip the piece to the opposite end and push the end that has been cut tight to the bed of the jointer. Slowly run the stock over the blade. It will begin to cut about 6" into the stock, and when finished there should be a thin $^1/_4$" thickness at the end. You will need to sand to fit.

step 26 Slide the pieces into the mortises in the crest rail and mark where they meet the back seat rail. At that line cut a $^1/_4$" half-lap-style cut. The shoulder created will rest on the rail.

step 27 Cut the seat/slat lock piece to size and nip the back edge corners at 45° for looks. Lay out the piece as you did the mortises in the crest rail and cut the dadoes $^1/_4$" deep. Glue and screw the front seat assembly into the notch in the rear legs.

Slide the slats into the crest rail and clamp the pieces, causing them to bow into the chair as shown. Add glue to the lock piece and attach it to the back seat rail with screws from the opposite side. Allow this to dry before removing the clamps.

step 28 Attach the corner blocks and seat braces to the inside of the rails with glue and screws. Set them at $^5/_8$" below the rail top. Cut the plywood subseat for the chair and apply the finish. I applied a coat of oil to enhance the grain of the tiger maple, sealed with a coat of shellac and sprayed with three coats of dull-rubbed-effect lacquer. If you are so inclined, you can upholster your seat or have it done professionally.

creating a bending form

Another option for creating a bending form can be found in the sidebar at the end of project eight.

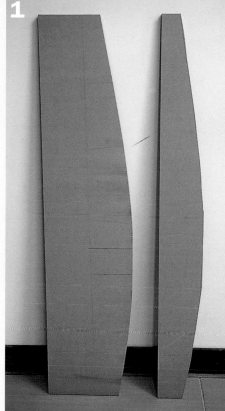

step 1 Make this form with medium-density fiberboard (MDF). Lay out the shape of the bend, leaving a flat area where the seat connects, onto a 12"-wide piece of MDF. Carefully cut to the line and smooth the cut. Rough-cut a second piece of MDF about 6" wide. Attach it to the first layer with glue and screws. Use a pattern bit with bottom-mount bearing to cut the second layer to match the first.

step 2 Repeat this process until you reach the necessary height of the form. In this case the form is $4\frac{1}{2}$", and six layers were needed. Add pieces to the back edge for support and clamping. The top layer should be 12" wide, as well.

step 3 Set the glued pieces into the form and clamp tightly.

BARBER'S-POLE BED

A few years ago I was walking through an antique flea market with my wife and we stumbled upon a set of four aged, wooden columns. Immediately an idea popped into my head. A barber's-pole bed! I kept that thought for years before I made good on the idea.

This is a fun project that will give you good methods to make a solidly built bed. There is a bit of simple lathe turning, simple joinery and an age-old method for assembling the bed that is still the best method used today — bed bolts!

This selection will keep you smiling throughout. The painting is a blast! Oh yeah, you get to use some of that high school math, as well.

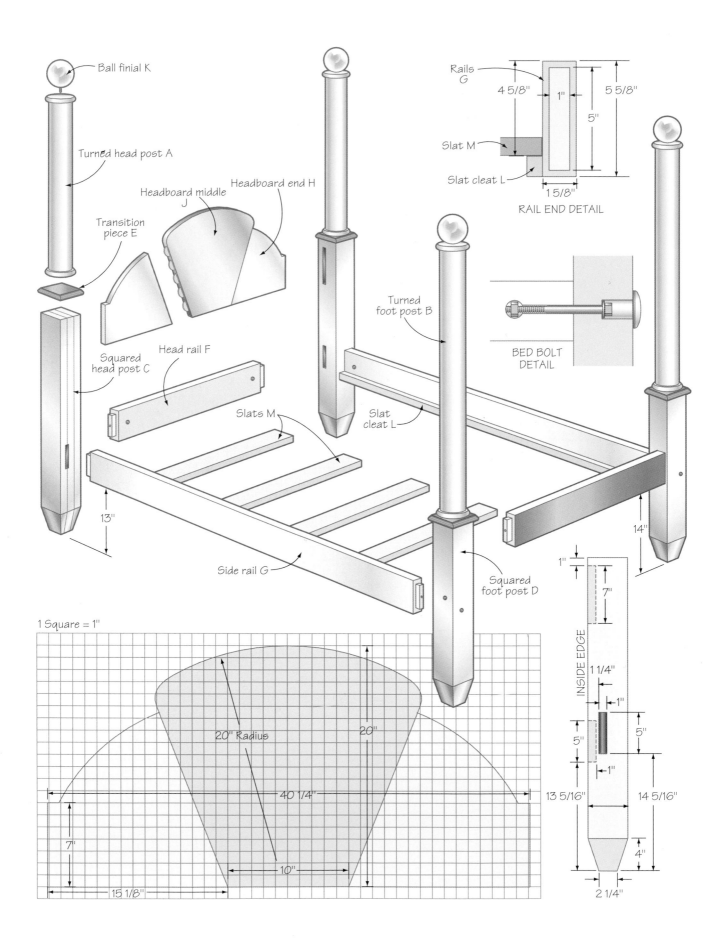

Ball finial K

Turned head post A

Headboard middle J

Headboard end H

Transition piece E

Squared head post C

Head rail F

Slats M

Side rail G

Rails G

4 5/8"

1"

5 5/8"

5"

Slat M

Slat cleat L

1 5/8"

RAIL END DETAIL

BED BOLT DETAIL

Turned foot post B

Slat cleat L

Squared foot post D

Turned foot post B

13"

14"

1 Square = 1"

20" Radius

20"

40 1/4"

7"

10"

15 1/8"

INSIDE EDGE

1"

7"

1 1/4"

1"

5"

5"

1"

13 5/16"

14 5/16"

4"

2 1/4"

inches (millimeters)

REFERENCE	QUANTITY	PART	STOCK	THICKNESS	(mm)	WIDTH	(mm)	LENGTH	(mm)	COMMENTS
A	2	turned head posts	poplar	$5^{1}/_4$	(133)	$5^{1}/_4$	(133)	27	(686)	glued to size from smaller pieces
B	2	turned foot posts	poplar	$5^{1}/_4$	(133)	$5^{1}/_4$	(133)	38	(965)	glued to size from smaller pieces
C	2	squared head posts	poplar	$4^{7}/_8$	(124)	$4^{7}/_8$	(124)	38	(965)	glued to size from smaller pieces
D	2	squared foot posts	poplar	$4^{7}/_8$	(124)	$4^{7}/_8$	(124)	27	(686)	glued to size from smaller pieces
E	4	transition pieces	poplar	$3/_4$	(19)	$5^{7}/_8$	(149)	$5^{7}/_8$	(149)	
F	2	head and foot rails	poplar	$1^{5}/_8$	(41)	$5^{5}/_8$	(143)	$40^{1}/_4$	(1022)	$5/_8$" (16) TBE
G	2	side rails	poplar	$1^{5}/_8$	(41)	$5^{5}/_8$	(143)	$76^{1}/_4$	(1936)	$5/_8$" (16) TBE
H	1	headboard end	poplar	$3/_4$	(19)	16	(406)	27	(686)	makes 2 pieces
J	1	headboard middle piece	poplar	$1^{1}/_8$	(28)	20	(508)	23	(584)	
K	4	ball finials	poplar	$4^{1}/_2$	(115)	$4^{1}/_2$	(115)	$4^{1}/_2$	(115)	
L	2	slat cleats	poplar	$3/_4$	(19)	1	(25)	$74^{1}/_2$	(1893)	
M	4	slats	poplar	$7/_8$	(22)	$3^{1}/_2$	(89)	$40^{3}/_4$	(1035)	

Note: TBE = tenon both ends.

hardware

8	7" (178mm) Bed bolts	item #H-73	Horton Brasses
6	Antique-finish bed bolt covers	item #BC-8	Horton Brasses
4	$5/_{16}$" x $2^{1}/_2$" (8mm x 64mm) Iron dowel screws		local hardware store
16	2" (51mm) Square-drive wood screws		local hardware store
	Glue		
	No. 8 × $1^{1}/_4$" (32mm) Screws		
	#20 Biscuits		
	Gold, blue, red and white paint		
	Posterboard		
	Lacquer		

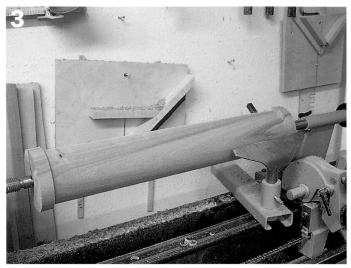

step 1 Begin this project by gluing the turned post pieces, square post pieces and ball finial blanks.

step 2 Select the four turned portions of the posts, two longer pieces for the foot posts and two shorter pieces for the head posts. Set the saw blade at 45° and cut away a portion of the posts that would have to be turned off at the lathe. Draw a circle on the end to show the cuts. Don't go inside the lines.

step 3 Mount the pieces in the lathe and turn the entire piece to 5¼" diameter. Mark the 1" beads at the top and bottom, then turn the center to 4¼" diameter.

step 4 Turn the beads on each piece, then turn the ball finials to size and sand each piece completely.

step 5 Mill the remaining pieces for the posts 4⅞" square. Cut the square portion to size and orient them as you would use them in the bed. Mark the appropriate faces for head, foot and side rails.

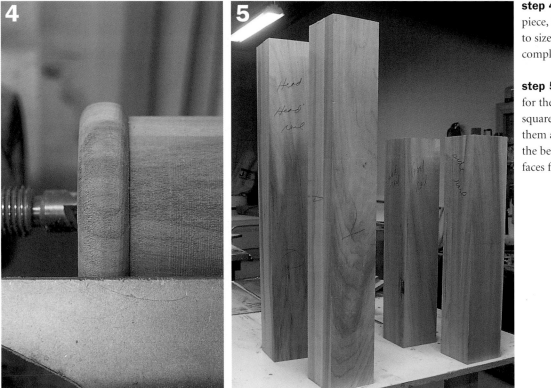

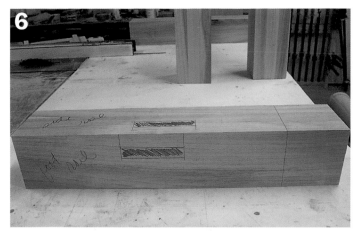

step 6 Mark the location of each of the mortises for the rails, as well as the cuff where the foot of each post will be tapered. Lay out the side rail mortise, then move 1" higher to lay out the foot and head mortise locations. This allows you to complete all other steps based on the center of each mortise and not have to offset the bolt locations.

step 7 Move to the mortiser and cut the mortises. The first run begins with the mortise edge set 1¼" from the inside corner.

step 8 Complete the mortise by readjusting the bit to cut a full 1"-wide mortise that is ¾" deep by 5" long.

step 9 With the rail mortises finished, cut the mortise for the headboard to slide into. This mortise is ¾" wide by 7" long by 1" deep and begins 1" from the top end of the square portion of the head posts.

step 10 Then, drill a 1⅛" hole that is 1¼" deep for the bed bolts. The hole should be exactly centered in the mortise from top to bottom and side to side. Make sure to center on the mortise that is on the direct opposite side from where you are drilling. Here you can see the result of offsetting the mortise location: The holes are automatically offset, as well. Change to a ⁷⁄₁₆" bit and complete the hole through the post into the mortise. This will act as a guide in a later step.

step 11 Next, create the tapering on the foot of each square post section. First, draw the lines on one side of the foot and cut to the lines on the band saw. Then draw the lines on the surface that was exposed in the first step and cut those lines on the band saw as well. Finally, sand the sides smooth.

step 12 Mill the transition pieces to size and mould the edge after you mark the center of the piece. I used a cove and bead bit, but your favorite edge will also work.

step 13 Predrill a hole for the 2" square-drive screw at the center of the transition piece. Attach the piece with the screw through that piece into the bottom center of the round posts. The location should be left from the lathe turning. When set, add an additional three screws to secure the piece to the post.

step 14 Next, position the upper section of the post onto the square lower section and attach with four screws, one at each corner.

step 15 Complete this operation on all four posts, remembering to fix the short turned sections to the long square pieces and vice versa.

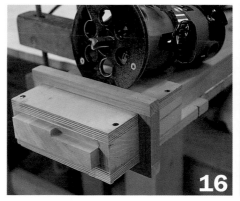

step 16 Now is the time to create the tenons on the ends of all rails. I make all my rails the same size ($1\frac{5}{8}$" × $5\frac{5}{8}$") and as a result, built a jig that slides on the end of my rails. Once in place, use a $\frac{3}{4}$" straight-cut bit set to cut $\frac{5}{16}$" into the rail. When run on all sides, the result is the 1" × 5" × $\frac{5}{8}$" tenon that matches the mortises made earlier.

step 17 Here is a better look at that jig and a completed tenon. The router base runs against the fence, and the bit cuts exactly at the edge of the jig. Simply set the jig to the desired tenon length ($\frac{5}{8}$") and run the cut. If you do not want to make the jig, you can cut these your favorite way, but remember, you have eight of these to complete.

step 18 With the rail tenons made, use a $1\frac{1}{2}$" Forstner bit and drill into the inside face of each rail $2\frac{3}{4}$" in from the shoulder of the tenon. Make the hole about $1\frac{3}{8}$" deep. At this time add the slat cleats by gluing and screwing the pieces to the inside bottom edge of the side rails only.

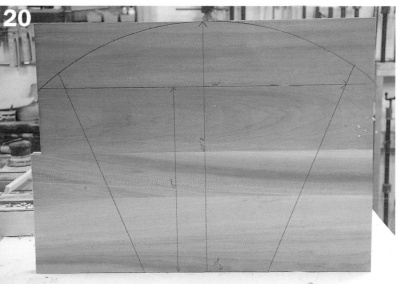

step 19 Set the posts and rails in place, clamp together with long pipe clamps and finish the hole for the bed bolts by using a $\frac{7}{16}$" bit (a long bit is required). Use the hole made in the posts (see step 10) as a guide and drill through the end of the rails into the holes created in the previous step. Drill all eight holes.

step 20 Next, we build the headboard. Begin by milling the pieces according to the materials list. Lay out and cut the $1\frac{1}{8}$"-thick middle section of the headboard. Cut the piece on the band saw, close to the line, then a pass over the jointer will clean and straighten the edge. Then cut and sand the top arc.

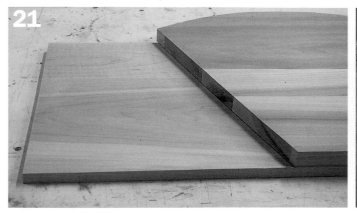

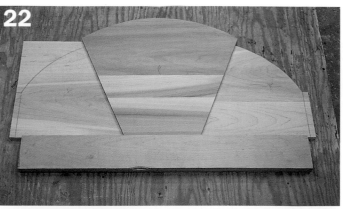

step 21 Mark the measurement for the end pieces. Set the middle section on the blank at that mark, align the bottom edges and mark the end piece for cutting. Flip the falloff of the piece to make the opposite end piece.

step 22 Lay out the 16" radius and cut, remembering to allow ⅝" for the tenon at both ends of the headboard. Set the pieces to a straightedge and make any small adjustments to the cuts.

step 23 Mark the back sides for the biscuit joinery. By making the cuts referenced to the back side, and not adjusting the cutter, you will end up with a smooth back and the difference in the thickness of the pieces will stand out in the front, creating a nice shadow line. Glue the headboard, and when dry, check the fit into the head post mortises. Make necessary adjustments at this time.

step 24 Sand all pieces to prep for paint. Attach the ball finials to the turned upper posts with the iron dowel screws.

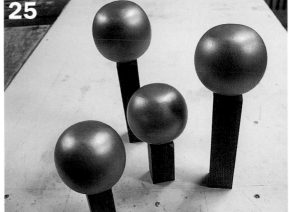

step 26 Here is where you will need those math skills. You will need to find the circumference of the post. Do this by multiplying the diameter of the posts by pi (3.142). The answer is the circumference (C). Divide that number by three. Cut a piece of posterboard to around 4" wide, then cut one end at a 45° angle. Measure that angled end the length of $C/3$. Cut the posterboard to that width. If you are building to my example, the posterboard should be cut to $3\frac{1}{8}$" wide. Next, set the angled end along the top edge of the bottom bead and slowly wrap the posterboard around the column while marking both edges with a pencil. Repeat the process by aligning the posterboard with one of the lines just marked and mark the opposite edge. This will divide the post into three equal sections that spiral around and up the post.

step 25 Time to begin the painting. Here you can see that the ball finials are painted with a gold paint. It will take a couple of coats. I found that I did not need a primer. At the same time you paint the finials, paint each of the four rails, as well.

step 27 Using masking tape, tape off one section of the spiral. Paint that blue, along with the base, transition piece and beads. It will take a couple of coats.

step 28 Repeat the taping and painting with both red and white colors to complete the posts. Paint the headboard. When all the paint is dry, spray a couple of coats of lacquer over the entire bed. That will seal the paint and make the piece easier to keep clean. Assembly is quick with the bed bolts. Then finish the project by adding the bolt covers over the six holes that can be seen with the bed against the wall. Set the slats into place on the slat cleats, add your mattress and box springs and enjoy a comfortable night's sleep.

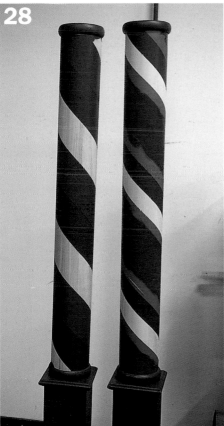

DESKEY SIDEBOARD

Donald Deskey was an American designer who helped establish what became known as the streamlined-modern style. This selection is based on a sideboard he designed in 1935.

It features a central bank of drawers with cupboard storage areas at either end. In this piece we are introduced to how shop-cut veneer can effectively enhance your work as we build the drawer fronts and doors. Also, we discover how the use of hardwood plywood can play a big part in your furniture.

I believe that this piece fits the idea that Mr. Deskey put forth and hope that it becomes a part of your portfolio, as well.

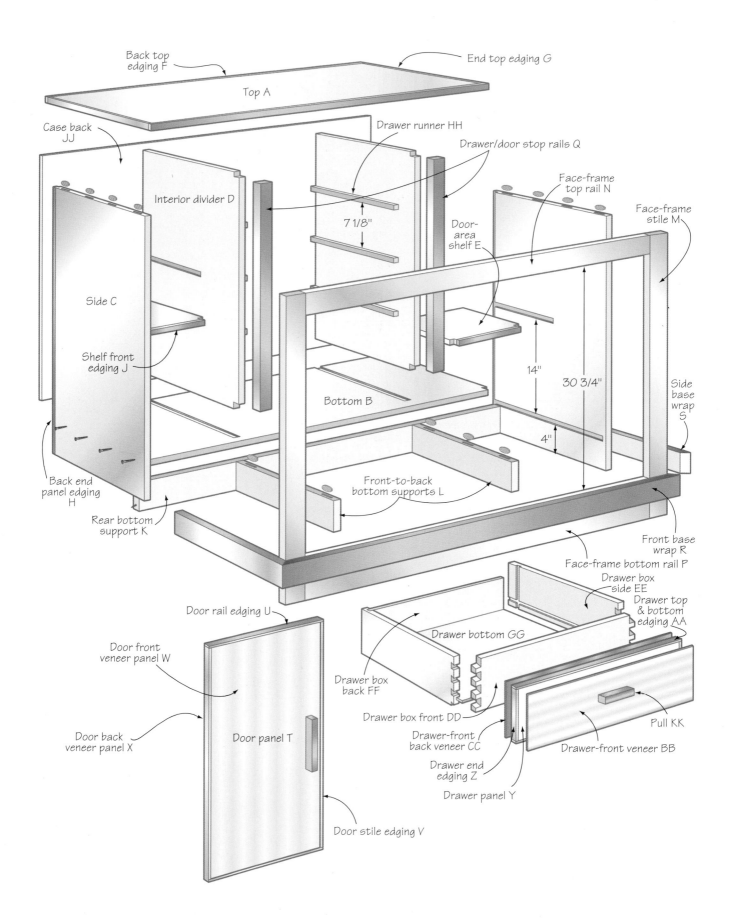

Back top edging F

End top edging G

Top A

Case back JJ

Drawer runner HH

Drawer/door stop rails Q

Interior divider D

Face-frame top rail N

Face-frame stile M

7 1/8"

Door-area shelf E

Side C

Shelf front edging J

14"

30 3/4"

Bottom B

Side base wrap S

4"

Back end panel edging H

Rear bottom support K

Front-to-back bottom supports L

Front base wrap R

Face-frame bottom rail P

Drawer box side EE

Drawer top & bottom edging AA

Door rail edging U

Drawer bottom GG

Door front veneer panel W

Drawer box back FF

Door panel T

Door back veneer panel X

Drawer box front DD

Pull KK

Drawer-front back veneer CC

Drawer-front veneer BB

Drawer end edging Z

Drawer panel Y

Door stile edging V

inches (millimeters)

REFERENCE	QUANTITY	PART	STOCK	THICKNESS	(mm)	WIDTH	(mm)	LENGTH	(mm)	COMMENTS
A	1	top	plywood	$3/4$	(19)	$19^{1}/_4$	(489)	$64^{1}/_2$	(1639)	does not include edge-banding
B	1	bottom	plywood	$3/4$	(19)	$18^{3}/_4$	(476)	64	(1626)	does not include edge-banding
C	2	sides	plywood	$3/4$	(19)	$19^{1}/_4$	(489)	$36^{1}/_4$	(920)	does not include edge-banding
D	2	interior dividers	plywood	$3/4$	(19)	$17^{7}/_8$	(454)	$31^{5}/_8$	(803)	
E	2	door-area shelves	plywood	$3/4$	(19)	$10^{1}/_2$	(267)	$18^{3}/_{16}$	(462)	less front edge
F	2	back top edging	cherry	$1/4$	(6)	$7/8$	(22)	65	(1651)	
G	2	end top edging	cherry	$1/4$	(6)	$7/8$	(22)	21	(533)	
H	2	back end panel edging	cherry	$1/4$	(6)	$7/8$	(22)	37	(940)	
J	2	shelf front edging	cherry	$1/2$	(13)	$3/4$	(19)	$18^{3}/_{16}$	(462)	
K	1	rear bottom support	plywood	$3/4$	(19)	4	(102)	$63^{1}/_2$	(1613)	
L	2	front-to-back bottom supports	plywood	$3/4$	(19)	4	(102)	18	(457)	
M	2	face-frame stiles	cherry	$3/4$	(19)	$1^{1}/_2$	(38)	$37^{1}/_{16}$	(942)	
N	1	face-frame top rail	cherry	$3/4$	(19)	$1^{1}/_2$	(38)	62	(1575)	
P	1	face-frame bottom rail	cherry	$3/4$	(19)	$4^{3}/_4$	(121)	62	(1575)	
Q	2	drawer and door stop rails	cherry	$15/16$	(24)	$1^{5}/_8$	(41)	$31^{1}/_2$	(800)	
R	1	front base wrap	cherry	$1/2$	(13)	$2^{3}/_4$	(70)	$66^{1}/_8$	(1679)	
S	2	side base wraps	cherry	$1/2$	(13)	$2^{3}/_4$	(70)	20	(508)	
T	2	door panels	Baltic birch ply	$5/8$	(16)	16	(406)	$29^{1}/_2$	(750)	
U	4	door rail edging	cherry	$1/2$	(13)	$3/4$	(19)	17	(432)	
V	4	door stile edging	cherry	$1/2$	(13)	$3/4$	(19)	$30^{1}/_2$	(775)	
W	2	door front veneer panels	cherry	$1/8$	(3)	$17^{1}/_4$	(438)	31	(787)	
X	2	door back veneer panels	paperback	*		$17^{1}/_4$	(438)	31	(787)	
Y	4	drawer panels	Baltic birch ply	$5/8$	(16)	$6^{5}/_8$	(168)	27	(686)	
Z	8	drawer end edging	cherry	$1/2$	(13)	$3/4$	(19)	$7^{5}/_8$	(194)	
AA	8	drawer top and bottom edgings	cherry	$1/2$	(13)	$3/4$	(19)	28	(711)	
BB	4	drawer-front front veneer panels	cherry	$1/8$	(3)	8	(203)	$28^{1}/_2$	(724)	
CC	4	drawer-front back veneer panels	paperback *			8	(203)	$28^{1}/_2$	(724)	
DD	4	drawer box fronts	poplar	$1/2$	(13)	$6^{7}/_8$	(174)	$26^{9}/_{16}$	(674)	
EE	8	drawer box sides	poplar	$1/2$	(13)	$6^{7}/_8$	(174)	17	(432)	
FF	4	drawer box backs	poplar	$1/2$	(13)	$6^{1}/_8$	(155)	$25^{13}/_{16}$	(656)	
GG	4	drawer bottoms	Birch birch ply	$1/2$	(13)	$16^{3}/_8$	(416)	26	(660)	
HH	6	drawer runners	poplar	$3/4$	(19)	1	(25)	17	(432)	
JJ	1	case back	plywood	$1/4$	(6)	36	(914)	64	(1626)	
KK	6	pulls	walnut	$7/8$	(22)	$7/8$	(22)	8	(203)	

hardware

2 pairs	$1^{1}/_2$" × $1^{1}/_2$" (38mm × 38mm) Finial tip butt hinges		item #41062		Rockler
	#20 Biscuits				
	Screws				
	No. 6 × $1^{1}/_4$" (32mm) Pocket screws				
	Finish nails				
	$3/4$" (19mm) Brad nails				
	Aniline dye stain				
	Lacquer				
Rare earth magnet (door catch):					
	4	Steel cups	item #99K32.52	Lee Valley	
	4	Washers	item #99K32.62	Lee Valley	
	4	Magnets	item #99K32.03	Lee Valley	

step 1 Begin here with the layout and cutting of the plywood pieces. You will need two sheets of $\frac{3}{4}$" and one sheet of $\frac{1}{4}$" hardwood plywood. Cut the pieces according to the materials list.

step 2 Mill the edging for the plywood and apply it to the rear edge of the sides and top, as well as the ends of the top. Nothing attaches to the front because we use a face frame. Make sure that the edging is centered on the plywood. Use the panels as cauls with a setup as shown.

step 3 For the ends of the top it is necessary to use a scrap piece of wood to spread the pressure.

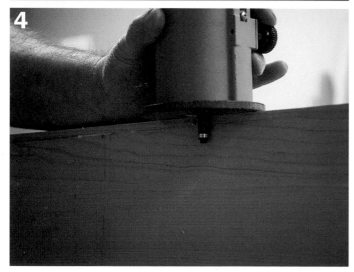

step 4 Next, take a flush-trim bit in the trim router and run both edges of the plywood.

step 5 Normally you could use a pattern bit; however, because of the undersizing of the hardwood plywood, I find it necessary to make a quick jig to accomplish the task. Attach two pieces of $\frac{1}{2}$" plywood, leaving a step as you can see in the photo.

Install the correct router bit to match the plywood thickness. Make a pass with the bit lowered enough to cut the bottom piece of plywood, using the top piece as a guide for the base plate. The result is a straightedge jig that can be set to the exact layout line.

step 6 Use the jig to rout the stop-dadoes for the interior dividers into the bottom panel. The cut does not extend through the front edge.

step 7 Then make the cuts into the side panels for the bottom and the shelves.

step 8 Next, match up the interior divider panels to the corresponding sides by aligning the top edge. Mark the location of the shelf dado and make those cuts.

step 9 Using a rabbeting bit, create the rabbets in the side panels at the rear, cutting away a portion of the solid edging.

step 10 With the same setup, make the rabbet in the top panel. Here, it is important to stay about ⅝" short of the ends of the panel.

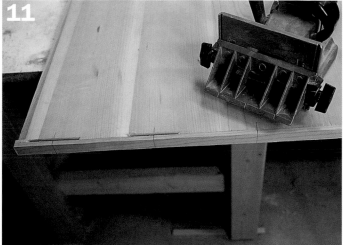

tip | Before cutting the slots into a case side that is to match to a top, add a few pieces of duct tape to the bed of the joiner. This helps to push the side slightly away from the edge, making certain to keep the top overhang.

step 11 Lay out and cut slots for the #20 biscuits. (If you find it easier, use an extended straightedge.)

step 12 Set the side into place with the top down and transfer the layout lines to the sides. With the face-side up, cut the matching biscuits. (See the tip.)

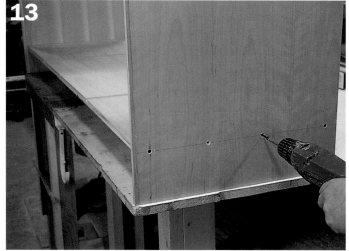

step 13 Begin assembling the case by sliding the bottom into the sides. Align the front edges and attach with screws through the sides. These screws will be covered later.

step 14 Place the biscuit into the side panels and test the fit of the top. Make any adjustments that might be necessary.

step 15 When ready, glue the top to the sides, clamp and let dry.

step 16 Install the rear bottom support by using pocket screws, then finish nail through the bottom into the support, aligning as you go.

step 17 Slide the interior dividers into place, remembering to have the shelf dadoes in the correct orientation. Use a square to position the divider and attach with pocket screws. Repeat the steps for the second divider.

step 18 Flip the case onto the top and begin the installation of the shorter front-to-back bottom supports. Here we are making the connection with biscuits. Clamp the support in place and use it as a guide to cut the slots into the underside of the bottom. Finally, glue the pieces to the bottom and fix the rear edge with screws through the rear support.

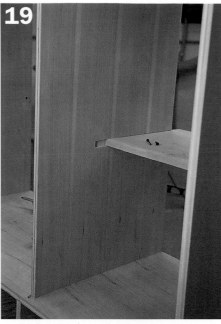

step 19 Glue the shelf front edging to the shelf and trim as we did the sides and top. Slide the shelf in the dado and attach with screws from the drawer area into the shelf. On the outside edge of the shelf, use a finish nail from the bottom up, through the shelf and into the side.

step 20 Next, cut the stiles for the face frame and clamp them into place. Place the top and bottom rails with a square-cut end against one stile and mark the final length of each rail. Assemble the face frame with pocket screws.

step 21 Lay out and cut the slots for biscuits, then attach the face-frame assembly to the case. When dry, use a cabinet scraper to level any needed areas.

step 22 Mill the material for the drawer runners and install them into the case. It helps to cut two spacers in setting the correct height.

step 23 Next, cut the door and drawer plywood to size. Mill the edging for the components and cut to size in order to fit around the plywood. Use 45° angle cuts at the corner of each component. Glue the pieces in place and allow to dry.

24

t i p | You can make your cauls quickly. Start with a 1¾"-square piece of stock that is 30" long. Set the jointer for about a ⅛" cut, start 3" from the center and make a pass over the blade. Turn the piece end for end and run that end over the blade. Now you are ready to clamp.

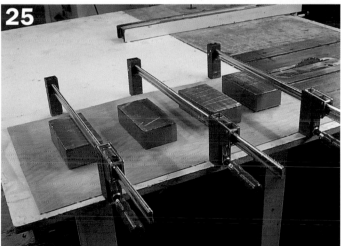

25

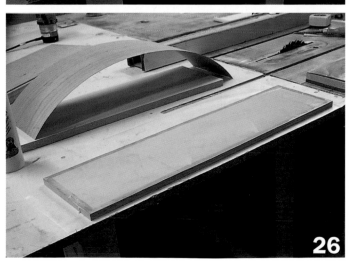

26

step 24 Select the lumber that will become your bookmatched door and drawer fronts. As you can see from the opening photo, using slices from the same board can have a dramatic effect on the piece. Try to choose the pieces for the door so that two slices will equal the width needed. Set up the band saw to slice your veneer with a ½" skip tooth blade. First, find the natural travel of your blade by cutting a straight line along a scrap piece. You will find that as you cut, your lumber will need to be moved to an angle. That is the natural cut of the blade. Mark that angle, then clamp an auxiliary fence at that angle. Flatten one side of the lumber and run a 90° face on the edge. Set the thickness of cut at ³⁄₁₆" and slice the necessary pieces.

step 25 For the door fronts, edge-glue your two pieces together, clamp lightly and weight the center with bricks. Wrap the bricks with duct tape to keep them from sticking or marring the surface. When dry, run the pieces for the two doors and four drawer fronts through the sander to prepare for veneering. Also, cut the purchased veneer for the back side of the components.

step 26 Stack your pieces in sequence. Spread glue onto the back side of the veneer front, then on both surfaces of the substrate, finally onto the back side of the purchased veneer.

step 27 Slide your sandwich between two pieces of melamine and attach spring clamps at the corners to hold everything in place. Position the cauls as shown and clamp the ends, thus squeezing the sandwich from the middle out. Replace the spring clamps with regular clamps and allow to dry. Use two sets of cauls on each door and one centered in each drawer front.

step 28 As you remove the doors and drawer fronts from the clamps, use the flush-trim bit to clean the edges, then sand smooth.

step 29 The thickness of the doors and drawer fronts will decide the final thickness of the stop rails that fit against the interior dividers. These pieces act as a stop for the doors and drawers. You want the drawers to be flush with the face frame.

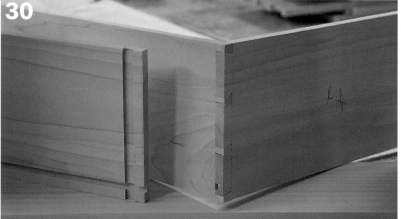

step 30 Build the drawer boxes next. The sides are joined to the front with dovetails, and the backs are set into dadoes in the sides with the tops even and simply nailed.

step 31 The ½" plywood drawer bottoms are rabbeted at the front and sides, then slid into the box and nailed into the drawer backs.

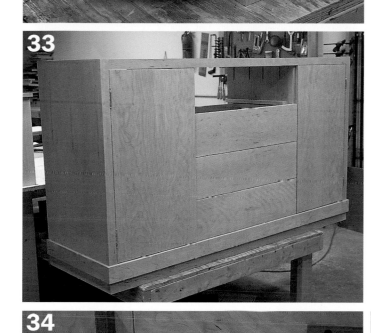

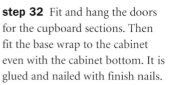

step 32 Fit and hang the doors for the cupboard sections. Then fit the base wrap to the cabinet even with the cabinet bottom. It is glued and nailed with finish nails.

step 33 Set the drawer box into the case. Use spacers to set the fronts, building off of the cabinet base. Hold the front in position with spring clamps and attach to the box with screws from the inside.

step 34 Mill the walnut for the handles. Set the jointer fence to 5° and run the stock over the blade. On the opposite side, repeat this step, creating a pull that is dovetail shaped when you view it from the end. Attach the pulls to the drawer fronts with screws and plug the holes. Attach the pulls to the doors with screws from the inside.

step 35 This piece is ready to go to the finish room. Take this time to install the rare earth magnets at the top and bottom of each door. Test the connection, then remove the parts and get ready to stain.

step 36 To finish this sideboard I selected a water-based aniline dye stain and lacquer top coat. After the finish is dry, nail the case back to the unit.

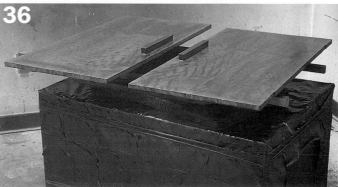

KRENOV-INSPIRED WINE CABINET

A cabinet on a stand is symbolic of the work of James Krenov. While true followers of his designs will take issue with some aspects of this project, I feel that the piece reflects his overall style. It is a fine introduction to Mr. Krenov's work, with a simplistic touch.

The cabinet has a straight-line appearance on the exterior that allows the hardwood to speak. You actually want to touch this piece! The inside, while it has a determined use, possesses those same lines. The contrasting dark-colored base elevates the cabinet to eye level and causes the piece to appear to float above the floor.

My hope is that this piece will intrigue you to look further into the designs of this master.

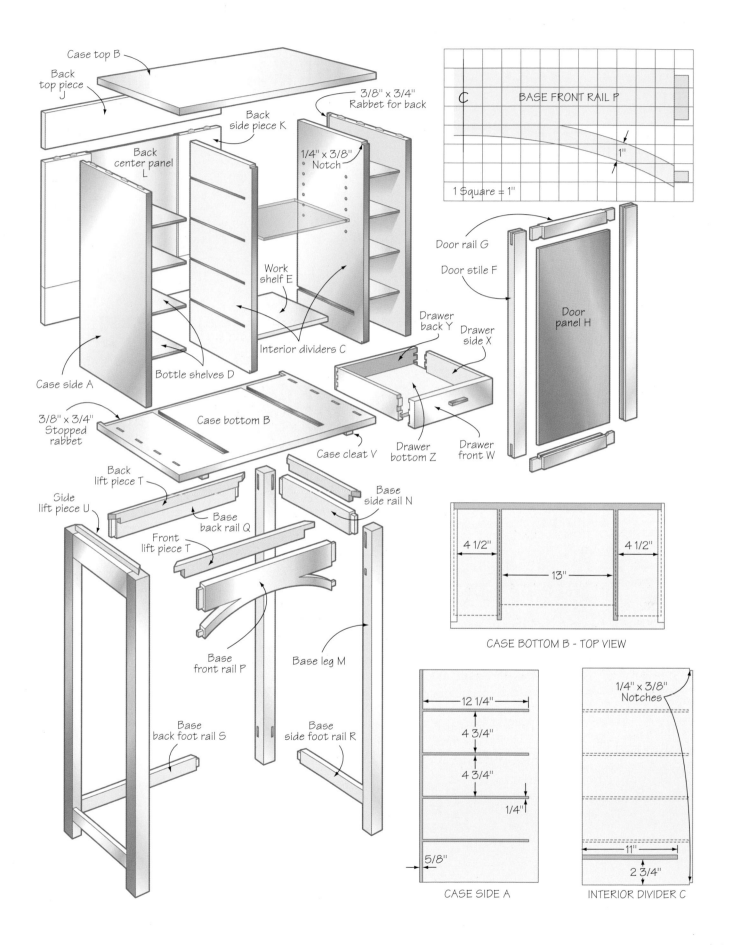

Case top B

Back top piece J

3/8" x 3/4" Rabbet for back

Back side piece K

Back center panel L

1/4" x 3/8" Notch

C   BASE FRONT RAIL P

1"

1 Square = 1"

Work shelf E

Door rail G

Door stile F

Door panel H

Case side A

Bottle shelves D

Interior dividers C

3/8" x 3/4" Stopped rabbet

Case bottom B

Drawer back Y

Drawer side X

Drawer bottom Z

Drawer front W

Case cleat V

Back lift piece T

Base back rail Q

Base side rail N

Side lift piece U

Front lift piece T

Base front rail P

Base leg M

Base back foot rail S

Base side foot rail R

CASE BOTTOM B – TOP VIEW

4 1/2"   13"   4 1/2"

CASE SIDE A

12 1/4"

4 3/4"

4 3/4"

1/4"

5/8"

INTERIOR DIVIDER C

1/4" x 3/8" Notches

11"

2 3/4"

inches (millimeters)

REFERENCE	QUANTITY	PART	STOCK	THICKNESS	(mm)	WIDTH	(mm)	LENGTH	(mm)	COMMENTS
A	2	case sides	bird's-eye maple	3/4	(19)	13 3/4	(349)	24 1/2	(623)	
B	2	case top and bottom	bird's-eye maple	3/4	(19)	14 1/2	(369)	24 3/4	(629)	
C	2	interior dividers	bird's-eye maple	1/2	(13)	12 3/4	(324)	25	(635)	
D	2	bottle shelves	walnut	1/4	(6)	12 1/4	(311)	20	(508)	cut to fit
E	1	work shelf	bird's-eye maple	1/2	(13)	11	(279)	13 1/2	(343)	
F	4	door stiles	bird's-eye maple	3/4	(19)	2	(51)	24 1/2	(623)	
G	4	door rails	bird's-eye maple	3/4	(19)	2	(51)	12 1/4	(311)	
H	2	door panels	walnut	1/4	(6)	8 7/8	(225)	21	(533)	
J	2	back top and bottom pieces	walnut	5/8	(16)	4 3/4	(121)	24	(610)	
K	2	back side pieces	walnut	5/8	(16)	6	(152)	16 1/2	(419)	
L	1	back center panel	bird's-eye maple	1/4	(6)	12 5/8	(321)	17 1/8	(435)	
M	4	base legs	walnut	1 1/2	(38)	1 3/4	(45)	38	(965)	
N	2	base side rails	walnut	3/4	(19)	4	(102)	13 1/4	(336)	3/4" (19) TBE
P	1	base front rail	walnut	3/4	(19)	6 1/4	(158)	23 1/2	(597)	3/4" (19) TBE
Q	1	base back rail	walnut	3/4	(19)	4	(102)	23 1/2	(597)	3/4" (19) TBE
R	2	base side foot rails	walnut	3/4	(19)	2	(51)	13 1/4	(336)	3/4" (19) TBE
S	1	base back foot rail	walnut	3/4	(19)	2	(51)	23 1/2	(597)	3/4" (19) TBE
T	2	front lift pieces	walnut	5/8	(16)	2	(51)	23 15/16	(608)	
U	2	side lift pieces	walnut	5/8	(16)	2	(51)	13 3/16	(335)	
V	2	case cleats	poplar	5/8	(16)	3/4	(19)	11 3/4	(298)	
W	1	drawer front	bird's-eye maple	3/4	(19)	2 5/8	(67)	12 7/8	(327)	
X	2	drawer sides	maple	7/16	(11)	2 5/8	(67)	10 1/4	(260)	
Y	1	drawer back	maple	7/16	(11)	2	(51)	12 7/8	(327)	
Z	1	drawer bottom	poplar	7/16	(11)	10	(254)	12 1/2	(318)	

Note: TBE = tenon both ends.

hardware

2 pairs	2" × 1 1/8" (51mm × 29mm) Self-aged door hinges	item #32941	Rockler
1	Door lock	item #LK-9	Horton Brasses
1	Antique-finish angled strike plate	item #SP-3	Horton Brasses
1	Antique-finish door catch	item #FB-10	Horton Brasses
4	1/4" (6mm) Brass shelf supports	item #33-894	Rockler
1	1/4" × 9" × 12 3/4" (6mm × 229mm × 324mm) Glass shelf		
	#20 Biscuits		
	Glue		
	1/4" × 1 1/8" × 2" (6mm × 28mm × 51mm) Shop-made drawer pull		
	Oil/varnish mixture		

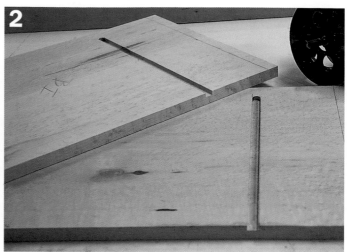

step 1 Begin this piece by milling the case sides, top and bottom. Cut the dadoes in the side pieces for the $\frac{1}{4}$" bottle shelves. These are stop-dadoes; they do not run completely through the front edge of the sides. For a straightedge jig, see project 11, step 5.

step 2 Next, cut the dadoes for the interior dividers into the top and bottom. Here you can use a $\frac{1}{2}$" pattern bit and straightedge. These are also stop-dado cuts.

step 3 Cut the $\frac{3}{4}$" × $\frac{3}{8}$" rabbet for the case back into the top and bottom by clamping a straightedge in position and using a pattern bit. These rabbets stop $\frac{5}{8}$" from the ends of the pieces. Cut the same-size rabbets into the sides. These can extend from end to end.

step 4 Set a square fence $\frac{7}{8}$" in from the end of the top layout and cut the slots for biscuits. Repeat the process for the bottom, as well.

step 5 Set the sides into position against the fence and transfer the layout lines onto the side faces. Lay the sides flat on the table, faceup, and cut the corresponding slots for the biscuit joint. When complete, glue the case together and check for square.

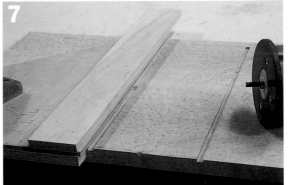

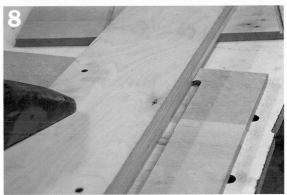

step 6 Mill the interior dividers and work shelf, leaving them a bit wide, then use a ½" beading bit to create the edge that will fit into the dadoes cut previously. Trim to final size.

step 7 Make sure to match the correct sides and cut the ¼" dadoes for the bottle shelves into the interior dividers.

step 8 On the opposite sides of the interior dividers, lay out and cut the ½" dado for the work shelf.

step 9 Slide the two dividers into the case, orienting the dadoes correctly.

step 10 Use a piece of pegboard to mark and drill the ¼" holes for the adjustable shelf clips for the glass shelf.

step 11 Next, mill the pieces for the bottle shelves, again a bit wide. To create the beaded edge, clamp the pieces to a straightedge and set the ¼" beading bit to correctly form the front of the shelves. Trim to final width, cut to correct length and slide the shelves into the case.

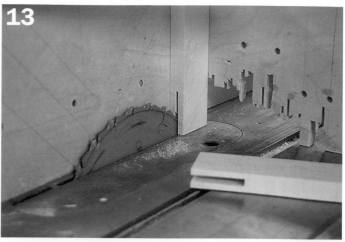

step 12 Next, we build the doors. The method of assembly is a slip joint, so all the pieces for the door frame are cut to full length. First, make the shoulder cut on the rails $\frac{1}{4}$" deep and the width of the stile (2"). Then remove the waste, leaving a $\frac{1}{4}$" tenon, as shown.

step 13 Reposition the blade to remove the corresponding waste in the stiles. You want a tight fit.

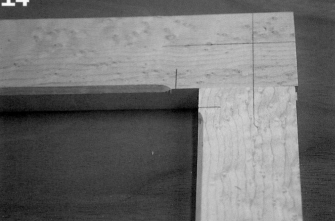

step 14 Slip the joint together, mark $\frac{1}{2}$" in from the connection and cut a slight chamfer on the edges as shown.

step 15 Because the ends of the tenons show at the door edge, you need to cut the $\frac{1}{4}$" groove for the door panels by adjusting the blade height to $\frac{3}{8}$" and mark the beginning and the end of the cut of the blade with masking tape. Set the fence at $\frac{1}{4}$" and drop-cut the rails and stiles. You can cut the stiles without the drop cut if you make sure that the groove is captured in the removed waste area.

step 16 Turn the rails so that the other face is against the fence and drop-cut to finish the grooves.

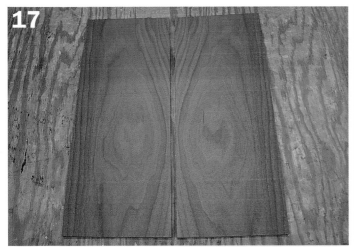

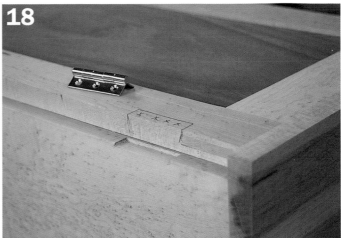

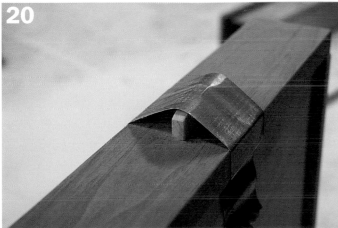

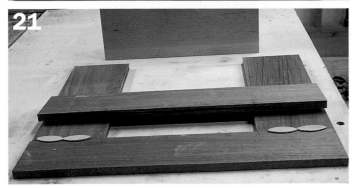

step 17 Cut the panels for the bookmatched door, then sand to the final thickness of ¹⁄₄". See project 11, step 24 for further details. Test the fit, then glue the door assemblies.

step 18 With the doors sanded, fit them to the case and install the hinges.

step 19 Next, install the door catch on the left-hand door so that the catch slides into the bottom, and the lock into the center of the right-hand door. Also, the angled strike plate fits adjacent to the lock in the left door.

step 20 Build the drawer to size. Here you see how I fashioned a clamp from duct tape to glue the shop-made pull into place. See project 6, steps 22 through 28 for more information on drawer construction.

step 21 Next, build the back assembly. Use the same steps to cut the groove for the back panel as we did for the door panels in steps 15 and 16. Then cut the biscuit joinery and assemble the back.

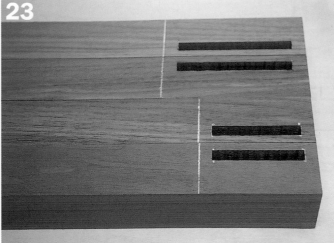

step 22 Now, we turn to the base. Mill your pieces to size and lay out the mortise cuts for all the rails. Cut the mortises for the foot rails in the center of the legs, adjusting for location and the differing widths of the legs.

step 23 Next, cut the mortises for the base rails ¼" in from the exterior edge of the legs. Remember to adjust the depth of cut with the differing widths of the legs and that the front rail mortises are different sizes.

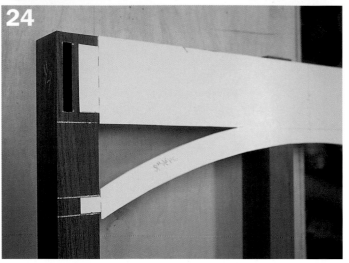

step 24 Make a posterboard template of the front rail to ensure that the lower mortise is placed correctly.

step 25 With the mortising complete, set up and cut the shoulder that defines the rabbeted foot.

step 26 Readjust the blade height and use a tenoning jig to complete the foot cut.

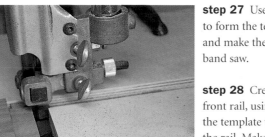

step 27 Use the same steps to form the tenons on the rails and make the final cuts at the band saw.

step 28 Create the tenon on the front rail, using the full 6¼". Use the template to lay out the cuts for the rail. Make and smooth the cuts for the front rail.

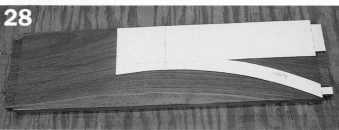

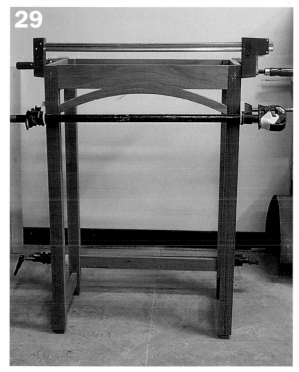

step 29 Assemble the two side sections of the base and then add the front and back rails to complete.

step 30 Next, cut the lift pieces to size. Cut 45° angles at the ends, then notch the pieces to fit over the legs. Complete all four corners.

step 31 With the lift pieces attached, cut the case cleats to size and attach to the bottom of the case. These should act as stops so that the case cannot slide from the base. I used them only at the ends. With that, this piece is ready to finish. I applied four coats of an oil/varnish mixture to build protection and sheen.

index

sources

BENDHEIM
61 Willett Street
Passaic, NJ 07055
800-835-5304
www.bendheim.com

DONALD DURHAM COMPANY
Box 804-E
Des Moines, IA 50304
www.waterputty.com

HORTON BRASSES INC.
Nooks Hill Road
P.O. Box 95
Cromwell, CT 06416
800-754-9127
www.horton-brasses.com

IRION LUMBER CO.
P.O. Box 954
Wellsboro, PA 16901-0954
570-724-1895
www.irionlumber.com

LEE VALLEY TOOLS LTD.
P.O. Box 1780
Ogdensburg, NY 13669
800-267-8735
www.leevalley.com

OLDE CENTURY COLORS
24656 Old Cleveland Road
South Bend, IN 46628
800-222-3092
www.oldecenturycolors.com

ROCKLER WOODWORKING & HARDWARE
4365 Willow Drive
Medina, MN 55340
800-279-4441
www.rockler.com

WOODCRAFT SUPPLY
P.O. Box 1686
Parkersburg, WV 26102
800-535-4482
www.woodcraft.com

WOODWORKER'S SUPPLY, INC.
Attn. Order Dept.
1108 North Glenn Road
Casper, WY 82601
800-645-9292
www.woodworker.com